THE MACMILLAN GUIDE TO

ENGLISH GRAMMAR

Rosalind Fergusson is a freelance editor and lexicographer and has compiled reference books and dictionaries for Chambers, Routledge, Penguin, Hamlyn, Oxford, and Bloomsbury.

Martin Manser is one of Britain's leading lexicographers, and has edited over twenty reference books, including dictionaries and word books for Oxford, Chambers, Bloomsbury, Guinness, and Penguin.

THE MACMILLAN GUIDE TO

ENGLISH GRAMMAR

Rosalind Fergusson
Martin H. Manser

MACMILLAN

First published 1998 by Macmillan

an imprint of Macmillan Publishers Ltd
25 Eccleston Place, London, SW1W 9NF
and Basingstoke

Associated companies throughout the world

ISBN 0333 67861 3

1 3 5 7 9 8 6 4 2

A CIP catalogue record for this book is available from the British Library

Typeset by Florencetype Ltd, Stoodleigh, Devon
Printed and bound in Great Britain by
Mackays of Chatham plc, Chatham, Kent

Contents

Introduction

Aims

This book on English grammar is a guide to how the English language works. It is aimed at native speakers of English who were never taught traditional grammar, or who have forgotten much of what they learnt. It will also be of interest to those who are learning English as a foreign or second language.

Presentation

The compilers and publishers have given considerable thought to the presentation of the *Macmillan Guide to English Grammar* in order to make the information as clear and accessible as possible.

The Quick-reference guide gives concise explanations of terms that may be unfamiliar to you. The main text is divided into chapters, each dealing with a particular aspect of English grammar. At the beginning of each chapter the topics covered in that chapter are listed. The topics are then explored mostly in two-page sections. Some sections are longer, in which case the symbol {CONTD} is used at the end of the second page. Boxed feature panels highlight noteworthy aspects of the use of grammar in everyday language and literature. We have also made extensive use of cross-references to direct you to other pages in the book where a subject is dealt with. The index lists both the subjects referred to and also particular examples of usage in one single alphabetical listing.

Note that the asterisk * is used in front of a word or sentence to show that this usage is not acceptable in standard English.

We hope that you will find this book a useful, interesting, and enjoyable guide to the structure of the English language.

Rosalind Fergusson
Martin H. Manser

Quick-reference guide
to grammatical terms

Here is a list of the grammar terms used in this book. Some of them will be familiar to you; others may not. Whenever you encounter in the book a grammatical word or phrase that you do not understand, it is hoped that you will find it in this list.

Each entry in this list contains a page number where you will find a fuller explanation of the term. Some entries also contain words or phrases in bold type. These are references to other entries in the list, where you will find more information.

abstract noun (p. 54) a noun that refers to a feeling, quality, etc., which you cannot see or touch: e.g. *idea, surprise, impatience, knowledge*. Compare **concrete noun**.

active voice (p. 158) a way of using a verb in which the subject is the person or thing that performs the action of the verb: e.g. *Caroline broke the window*. Compare **passive voice**.

adjectival noun (p. 102) a noun used as an adjective before another noun: e.g. *village* in *the village church*, or *milk* in *milk bottles*.

adjective (p. 96) a word that gives you more information about a noun or pronoun, telling you what someone or something is like, etc.: e.g. *large, green, impossible, complete, old-fashioned, Spanish*.

adjective phrase (p. 108) a group of words containing an adjective and other words that tell you more about it: e.g. *too hot; deep enough; reluctant to help; very fond of children*.

adjunct (p. 180) an adverbial that relates to the verb or to the whole sentence: e.g. *in a taxi* in *She left the station in a taxi*, or *last week* in *He was made redundant last week*. Compare **conjunct, disjunct, subjunct**.

adverb (p. 172) a word that gives you more information about a verb, adjective, etc., telling you when, where, how, etc.: e.g. *tomorrow, often, here, away, out, slowly, generously, very*.

adverb clause (p. 173) any subordinate clause, with or without a verb, used adverbially: e.g. *when he found out*; *while washing the car*; *if possible*.

adverbial (p. 34; p. 173) a part of a clause or sentence that provides further information, usually about the verb: e.g. *suddenly* in *he left suddenly*, or *in a taxi* in *she left in a taxi*. Adverbials include adverbs, adverb phrases, adverb clauses, prepositional phrases, etc.

adverb phrase (p. 173) a phrase consisting of a head adverb with other words before and/or after it: e.g. *rather badly*; *strangely enough*; *very fast indeed*; *as often as possible*.

agreement = concord.

apposition (p. 92) the relationship between two noun phrases that follow each other: e.g. *Canberra* and *the capital of Australia* in *Canberra, the capital of Australia*.

appositive clause (p. 93) a clause that follows an abstract noun such as *fact*, *idea*, *thought*, *decision*, etc., and tells you what the fact (or idea, etc.) is: e.g. *that I am unemployed* in *the fact that I am unemployed*.

article (p. 80) any of the words *a*, *an*, or *the*. See also **definite article**, **indefinite article**, **zero article**.

aspect (p. 164) the form of a verb that tells you whether the action or state it refers to is complete or still in progress. See also **perfect aspect**, **progressive aspect**.

attributive (p. 96) (of an adjective) coming before the noun: e.g. *good* in *a good idea*, or *large* in *the large garden*. Compare **postpositive**, **predicative**.

auxiliary verb (p. 146) a verb like *is*, *have*, *do*, *will*, *should*, *could*, *may*, etc., used in front of the **main verb** in a verb phrase: e.g. *had* in *had opened*, or *were* in *were watching*. See also **modal verb**, **primary verb**.

back-formation (p. 169) the process of forming a new word by removing the ending from another: e.g. *self-destruct* from *self-destruction*; *liaise* from *liaison*.

base form (p. 136) the form of a verb with no added endings, used in the infinitive, in commands, etc.: e.g. *be*, *look*, *come*, *break*.

cardinal numeral (p. 82) any of the words *one*, *two*, *three*, *sixteen*, *twenty-four*, *nine hundred*, etc. Compare **ordinal numeral**.

case (p. 66; p. 128) a system in which nouns, pronouns, etc., change their form according to the way they are used within a sentence: e.g. *Jane/Jane's*; *I/me*. See also **common case**, **genitive**, **objective**, **subjective**.

central adjective (p. 96) an adjective that can be used both attributively and predicatively: e.g. *huge* in *a huge dog* and *the dog was huge*. Compare **peripheral adjective**.

central determiner (p. 78) a determiner such as *a/an*, *the*; *my*, *your*, etc.; *this*, *that*, etc.; *what*, *which*, *whose*; *each*, *some*, *any*, *no*, etc. See also **postdeterminer**, **predeterminer**.

clause (p. 29) a part of a sentence that usually contains a verb: e.g. *we left* and *when the show was over* in the sentence *We left when the show was over*. See also **finite clause**, **main clause**, **non-finite clause**, **subordinate clause**, **verbless clause**.

cleft sentence (p. 218) a sentence that has been split into two clauses for emphasis: e.g. *It was Jane who was playing the piano* (instead of *Jane was playing the piano*).

collective noun (p. 62) a noun that refers to a group of people, animals, etc.: e.g. *committee*, *herd*, *flock*, *team*.

comment clause (p. 210) a short clause that you add to show your attitude to what you are saying: e.g. *you see*; *I think*; *what's more*; *to be honest*.

common case (p. 66) the form of any noun that is not in the **genitive** case; e.g. *Jane*, *doctor*, *students*.

common noun (p. 50) any noun that is not a **proper noun**: e.g. *book*, *child*, *idea*, *patience*.

comparative (p. 100; p. 173) (of the form of an adjective or adverb) used to compare two things, people, events, etc.: e.g. *richer*, *more reliable*, *more urgently*. Compare **superlative**.

comparative clause (p. 208) a clause used when you are comparing people or things: e.g. *older than I am* in *Jack is older than I am*.

complement (p. 33) a word or phrase – usually an adjective or noun – that follows a copular verb such as *be*, *become*, *feel*, etc.: e.g. *ill* in *he felt ill*, or *my niece* in *Anna is my niece*. See also **object complement**, **prepositional complement**, **subject complement**.

complex preposition (p. 188) a preposition that consists of two or more words: e.g. *according to*, *because of*, *as well as*, *in addition to*. Compare **simple preposition**.

complex sentence (p. 203) a sentence that contains a main clause and a subordinate clause beginning with *while*, *before*, *if*, etc.: e.g. *We left when the show was over*. Compare **compound sentence**.

compound adjective (p. 106) an adjective made up of two or more other words, at least one of which is usually an adjective: e.g. *seasick*; *paper-thin*; *red-haired*; *well-known*.

compound adverb (p. 172) an adverb that consists of two words joined together: e.g. *everywhere, somehow, thereupon, hereby*. Compare **simple adverb**.

compound noun (p. 70) a noun made up of two or more other words, at least one of which is usually a noun: e.g. *air force; bookshop; father-in-law; passer-by*.

compound sentence (p. 202) a sentence that contains two main clauses linked by *and, or, but*, etc.: e.g. *The cat ran across the road and the dog chased it*. Compare **complex sentence**.

concord (p. 36) the relationship between two or more words or phrases that must have the same number, gender, etc., for the sentence to be grammatical: e.g. *boy* and *has* (both singular) in *the boy has a dog*.

concrete noun (p. 54) a noun referring to something that you can see, touch, etc.: e.g. *book, child, mud, granite*. Compare **abstract noun**.

conjunct (p. 183) an adverbial that provides a link between clauses, sentences, or paragraphs: e.g. *therefore, for example, firstly, on the other hand*. Compare **adjunct, disjunct, subjunct**.

conjunction (p. 196) a word or phrase that links two clauses or other parts of a sentence: e.g. *and, or, but, when, if, although, because*. See also **coordinating conjunction, subordinating conjunction.**

continuous aspect = progressive aspect.

contraction (p. 214) shortening a word and attaching it to the word before, or a word formed in this way: e.g. *n't* for *not* in *isn't*; *'re* for *are* in *you're*; *'d* for *had* or *would* in *he'd*.

conversion (p. 25) coining new nouns, verbs, etc., by adopting words from different word classes: e.g. *a find* (from *to find*); *to ship* (from *a ship*).

coordinating conjunction (p. 196) a conjunction that links parts of a sentence that have the same status: e.g. *and* in *cold and damp; or* in *Would you like tea or coffee?; but* in *I speak French but I don't speak German*. Compare **subordinating conjunction**.

coordination (p. 204) the relationship or linking of parts of a sentence that have the same status, usually with a coordinating conjunction. Compare **subordination**.

coordinator = coordinating conjunction.

copular verb (p. 33; p. 151) a verb like *be, become, seem, grow, feel, sound*, etc., that links its subject to a complement: e.g. *is* in *the water is hot*, or *feel* in *I feel a fool*.

correlatives (p. 197) conjunctions used in pairs: e.g. *both . . . and; either . . . or; if . . . then*.

countable noun (p. 52) a noun that can be made plural: e.g. *book/books*, *child/children*, *dream/dreams*, *theory/theories*. Compare **uncountable noun**.

count noun = **countable noun**.

defining = **restrictive**.

definite article (p. 80) the word *the*. Compare **indefinite article**.

demonstrative (p. 120) (referring to) any of the words *this*, *that*, *these*, or *those*, used to distinguish between items.

dependent clause = **subordinate clause**.

derivation (p. 19) the way new words are formed by adding prefixes, suffixes, etc.: e.g. *happy/unhappy*, *break/breakable*.

determiner (p. 76) a word that comes before a noun and tells you how much, how many, which, whose, etc.: e.g. *a*, *the*, *my*, *your*, *this* (in *this car*), *whose* (in *whose bag*), *two* (in *two dogs*), *some* (in *some money*), *many* (in *many people*).

dialect (p. 20) the form of English spoken by a particular group of people, usually in a particular region of the country.

directive (p. 40) a clause or sentence that is a command, instruction, request, etc.: e.g. *Shut the door*!

direct object (p. 32) the word or phrase – often a noun or pronoun – that is directly affected by the action of the verb: e.g. *the ball* in *the girl kicked the ball*, or *the bone* in *he threw the dog a bone*. See also **indirect object**, **object**.

direct speech (p. 220) a way of reporting speech in which you repeat the actual words used: e.g. *'You're too late,' they told us*. Compare **indirect speech**.

disjunct (p. 182) an adverbial that provides a comment or observation on the style or content of a clause or sentence: e.g. *personally* in *Personally, I don't believe a word of it*. Compare **adjunct**, **conjunct**, **subjunct**.

ditransitive (p. 155) (of a verb) used with a direct object and an indirect object: e.g. *gave* in *I gave the child a present*. See also **transitive**.

double negative (p. 167) the use of two negative elements in a single sentence: e.g. *I didn't say nothing*.

dual gender (p. 65; p. 126) (of some nouns, pronouns, etc.) using the same form to refer to both sexes: e.g. *we*, *them*, *child*, *parent*, *teacher*, *cat*, *spider*.

-ed form (p. 139) the form of a verb that usually consists of the **base form** plus the ending *-ed*, used in the past tense and as the past participle: e.g. *looked*, *played*, *raced*, *tried*.

ellipsis (p. 213) leaving out part of a sentence, usually to avoid repetition: e.g. not repeating *finished* at the end of the sentence *I thought I'd finished but I hadn't*.

equivalence (p. 209) comparison to the same degree, using the structure *as . . . as*: e.g. *as much money as I need*. Compare **non-equivalence**.

exclamation (p. 41) a clause or sentence that expresses surprise, pleasure, anger, etc.: e.g. *How quiet they are!*

existential *there* (p. 217) the use of *there* as a 'dummy' subject, usually for emphasis, as in *There was no carpet on the floor*.

extraposition (p. 219) moving a clause to the end of a sentence for emphasis: e.g. *It is a mystery why he left* (instead of *Why he left is a mystery*).

feminine (p. 64; p. 126) (of some nouns, pronouns, etc.) usually referring to a female person or animal: e.g. *she, her, woman, girl, heroine, princess, hen, cow*. Compare **masculine**.

finite clause (p. 143) a clause that contains a finite verb phrase: e.g. *he drives a red car; if you had brought an umbrella*. Compare **non-finite clause**.

finite verb (p. 142) a verb used in the present tense, past tense, etc.: e.g. *belong* in *they belong to me*, or *walked* in *we walked home*. Compare **non-finite verb**.

finite verb phrase (p. 142) a verb phrase that contains a finite verb: e.g. *is wearing* in *she is wearing trousers*. Compare **non-finite verb phrase**.

first person (p. 114) being or including the person who is talking: e.g. the first person pronouns *I, me, myself, we, us, ourselves*, etc.

fronting (p. 217) moving something to the front of a sentence to make it stand out, as in *Down the hill she ran*.

gender (p. 64; p. 126) (of some nouns, pronouns, etc.) being **masculine** or **feminine**.

genitive (p. 66; p. 128) (referring to) the case or form of a noun, pronoun, etc. when it is used to show possession: e.g. *Jane's, doctor's, students'; my, mine, their, theirs, whose*.

gerund (p. 138) a rather old-fashioned name for the **-*ing* form** of a verb used as a noun: e.g. *smoking* in *smoking is forbidden*.

gradable (p. 97) (of an adjective) that can be used with words like *very, too, slightly*, etc., or in comparative and superlative forms: e.g. *expensive* in *a very expensive meal*, or *old* in *an older house*. Compare **non-gradable**.

head adjective (p. 108) the main adjective in an adjective phrase: e.g. *fond* in *very fond of children*, or *brown* in *dark brown*.

head noun (p. 72) the main noun in a noun phrase: e.g. *intentions* in *all our good intentions*, or *shop* in *the shop on the corner*.

imperative mood (p. 40; p. 157) the way a verb is used in commands, instructions, requests, etc.: e.g. *come* in *Come here!*, or *take* in *Take a seat*. Compare **indicative mood, subjunctive mood**.

indefinite article (p. 80) the word *a* or *an*. Compare **definite article**.

indefinite pronoun (p. 124) any of the set of pronouns *everything*, *everybody*, *everyone*, *something*, *anybody*, *no one*, etc., or a pronoun expressing quantity, such as *all* (in *all were destroyed*), *some* (in *some of the books are missing*), etc.

independent clause = main clause.

indicative mood (p. 156) the way a verb is used in statements or questions of fact: e.g. *have* in *I have no children*, or *are* in *Are these your car keys?* Compare **imperative mood, subjunctive mood**.

indirect object (p. 32) the word or phrase – often a noun or pronoun – that is indirectly affected by the action of the verb: e.g. *the dog* in *he threw the dog a bone*. See also **direct object, object**.

indirect speech (p. 220) a way of reporting speech in which you do not repeat the actual words used: e.g. *They told us that we were too late*. Compare **direct speech**.

infinitive (p. 143) the base form of the verb (i.e. without added endings), often preceded by *to*, used after a verb, adjective, etc.: e.g. *fall* in *she saw him fall*, or *to understand* in *it is hard to understand*.

inflection (p. 19) the way words change to show differences of tense, number, person, gender, etc.: e.g. *play/played*, *car/cars*, *am/is/are*, *he/she*.

-ing form (p. 138) the form of a verb that usually consists of the **base form** plus the ending *-ing*, used as the present participle, and sometimes as a noun or adjective: e.g. *being, looking, smoking, worrying*.

intensifier (p. 178) an adverb that tells you that something is more or less intense, great, strong, etc.: e.g. *very, extremely, too, rather, slightly*.

interjection (p. 42) an exclamatory sound that you make to show surprise, admiration, pain, disgust, etc.: e.g. *Wow!, Ouch!, Ugh!*

interrogative (p. 120) (referring to) any ***wh*-word** used to ask a question: e.g. *how, what, when, where, which, who, whom, whose, why*.

intonation (p. 228) varying the pitch of your voice to show that you are asking a question, to express emotion, etc.

intransitive (p. 154) (of a verb) used without a direct object: e.g. *appeared* in *the moon appeared*, or *fell* in *leaves fell from the trees*. Compare **transitive**.

invariable noun (p. 60) a noun that is either always singular or always plural: e.g. *aerobics, cattle, news, scissors*. Compare **variable noun, zero plural**.

inversion (p. 218; p. 222) changing the normal order of subject and verb, as in a question, for emphasis, or in direct speech: e.g. *Are you cold?*; *Out came the sun*; *'No,' replied Jack*.

irregular (p. 56; p. 135) that does not follow the usual pattern for words of its class or type: e.g. *feet* is an irregular plural form; *break* is an irregular verb. Compare **regular**.

linking verb = copular verb.

main clause (p. 29; p. 202) a clause that sounds complete and that can stand alone as a sentence, e.g. *we can go to the cinema* in the sentence *If it rains we can go to the cinema*. Compare **subordinate clause**.

main verb (p. 134) in a verb phrase, the word that expresses the meaning: e.g. *opened* in *had opened* or *should have opened*. Compare **auxiliary verb**.

major sentence (p. 28) a sentence that contains a finite verb (together with any necessary subject, object, etc.) and that sounds complete: e.g. *I opened the door*. Compare **minor sentence**.

masculine (p. 64; p. 126) (of some nouns, pronouns, etc.) usually referring to a male person or animal: e.g. *he, him, man, boy, hero, prince, cock, bull*. Compare **feminine**.

mass noun = uncountable noun.

minor sentence (p. 28) a word or string of words that expresses a complete thought or message, but that does not have to contain a finite verb: e.g. *What a pity!* Compare **major sentence**.

modal verb (p. 148) a verb that you can only use as an auxiliary verb: e.g. *will, would, shall, should, can, may, must*. Compare **primary verb**.

modifier (p. 84; p. 108) a **premodifier** or **postmodifier**.

mood (p. 156) see **indicative mood, subjunctive mood, imperative mood**.

multiple sentence (p. 29; p. 202) a sentence that contains more than one clause, and that can be broken into two or more sentences: e.g. *The soup is cold but the coffee is hot*. Compare **simple sentence**. See also **complex sentence, compound sentence**.

multi-word verb (p. 152) a verb that you use with an adverb or a preposition (or both) to form a complete unit of meaning: e.g. *let down*, meaning 'disappoint'; *look after*, meaning 'take care of'. See also **phrasal-prepositional**

verb, phrasal verb, prepositional verb.

negation (p. 166) the grammatical process of contradicting or denying the truth of a statement.

negative (p. 166) being or containing a word used in **negation**: e.g. *never* is a negative word; *I am not a psychiatrist* is a negative statement. See also **double negative**.

nominal adjective (p. 98) an adjective used as a noun: e.g. *homeless* in *a hostel for the homeless*, or *impossible* in *to attempt the impossible*.

non-count noun = **uncountable noun**.

non-defining = **non-restrictive**.

non-equivalence (p. 209) comparison to a higher or lower degree, using the structures *more . . . than*, *less . . . than*, etc.: e.g. *She is more talented than her father was*; *I had less time than I thought I had*. Compare **equivalence**.

non-finite clause (p. 143) a clause that contains a non-finite verb phrase: e.g. *to solve this problem*; *having forgotten the number*. Compare **finite clause**.

non-finite verb (p. 142) a verb used in the infinitive, or as a present or past participle: e.g. *leaving* in *on leaving the restaurant*. Compare **finite verb**.

non-finite verb phrase (p. 143) a verb phrase that consists of one or more non-finite verbs and does not contain a finite verb: e.g. *having been invited* in *having been invited to their wedding*. Compare **finite verb phrase**.

non-gradable (p. 97) (of an adjective) that cannot be used with words like *very*, *too*, *slightly*, etc., or in comparative and superlative forms: e.g. *impossible*, *perfect*, *unique*. Compare **gradable**.

non-restrictive (p. 88; p. 92) (of a relative clause, noun phrase in apposition, etc.) containing incidental information that can be left out: e.g. *which needs repairing* in *The computer, which needs repairing, is over there*. Compare **restrictive**.

noun (p. 48) a word for a thing, feeling, state, person, animal, place, etc.: e.g. *car, circle, happiness, freedom, nurse, Jack, dog, Europe*.

noun phrase (p. 72) a word or group of words that contains a noun or pronoun and that may be the subject, object, complement, etc., of a clause or sentence: e.g. *the old car*; *all our good intentions*; *cats* or *mice* in *cats chase mice*; *I* and *an English teacher* in *I am an English teacher*.

number (p. 56; p. 114) (of nouns, pronouns, etc.) being **singular** or **plural**.

numeral (p. 82) a **cardinal numeral** or an **ordinal numeral**.

object (p. 32) the word or phrase – often a noun or pronoun – that usually comes after the verb: e.g. *the ball* in *the girl kicked the ball*. See also **direct object**, **indirect object**. Compare **subject**.

object complement (p. 34) a **complement** that provides information about the object of a verb: e.g. *green* in *the shampoo turned her hair green*. Compare **subject complement**.

objective (p. 129) (referring to) the case or form of pronoun when it is used as the object of a verb or after a preposition: e.g. *me, him, her, us, them, whom*. Compare **subjective**.

ordinal numeral (p. 82) any of the words *first, second, third, fourteenth, fifty-sixth, seven thousandth*, etc. Compare **cardinal numeral**.

participial adjective (p. 102) an adjective that has the same form as a present or past participle: e.g. *interesting, worrying, isolated, broken*.

participle (p. 145) a **present participle** or a **past participle**.

particle (p. 152) the adverb or preposition that forms part of a **multi-word verb**.

part of speech = **word class**.

passive voice (p. 158) a way of using a verb in which the subject is the person or thing that receives the action of the verb: e.g. *The window was broken by Caroline*. Compare **active voice**.

past participle (p. 145) the **-ed** form (or irregular equivalent) of a verb used with *have* to express past time, with *be* to form the passive voice, etc.: e.g. *broken* in *she has broken her promise*, or *cleaned* in *the rooms are cleaned every day*.

past perfect (p. 164) the **aspect** of a verb that consists of the verb *have* in the past tense (i.e. had) followed by a past participle: e.g. *had worked, had seen*. Compare **present perfect**.

past progressive (p. 165) the **aspect** of a verb that consists of the verb *be* in the past tense (i.e. *was/were*) followed by a present participle: e.g. *was working, were seeing*. Compare **present progressive**.

past tense (p. 161) see **simple past tense**.

perfect aspect (p. 164) the **aspect** of a verb that consists of the verb *have* followed by a past participle: e.g. *has worked, had seen*. See also **past perfect**, **present perfect**.

perfective aspect = **perfect aspect**.

peripheral adjective (p. 97) an adjective that can be used either attributively or predicatively, but not both: e.g. *utter* in *utter incompetence*, or *asleep* in *the baby is asleep*. Compare **central adjective**.

person (p. 114) see **first person**, **second person**, **third person**.

personal pronoun (p. 114) any of the pronouns *I*, *me*, *you*, *he*, *him*, *she*, *her*, *it*, *we*, *us*, *they*, *them*, or a related **possessive** or **reflexive pronoun**.

phrasal-prepositional verb (p. 153) a **multi-word verb** that has two particles – an adverb and a preposition: e.g. *make up for*, meaning 'compensate for'.

phrasal verb (p. 152) a **multi-word verb** that has an adverb as its particle: e.g. *let down*, meaning 'disappoint'. (The term phrasal verb is sometimes used to cover all three types of multi-word verb.)

plural (p. 56) referring to more than one person, thing, etc.: e.g. *hats* is a plural noun; *those* is a plural pronoun; *are* is a plural verb in the sentence *We are bored*. Compare **singular**.

possessive (p. 118) (referring to) any of the set of words that show personal possession: i.e. *my*, *mine*, *your*, *yours*, *his*, *her*, *hers*, *its*, *our*, *ours*, *their*, *theirs*.

postdeterminer (p. 79) a determiner that can come after the **central determiner** in a noun phrase: e.g. *fifth* in *the fifth time*, or *many* in *our many problems*. Compare **predeterminer**.

postmodifier (p. 86; p. 109) in a noun phrase or adjective phrase, a word or phrase that follows the head noun, pronoun, or adjective and tells you more about it: e.g. *above* in *the sky above*, or *to help* in *reluctant to help*. Compare **premodifier**.

postpositive (p. 96) (of an adjective) coming straight after a noun or pronoun: e.g. *famous* in *nobody famous*, or *proper* in *the village proper*. Compare **attributive**, **predicative**.

predeterminer (p. 78) a determiner that can come before the **central determiner** in a noun phrase: e.g. *half* in *half an hour*, or *all* in *all the music*. Compare **postdeterminer**.

predicate (p. 35) everything that follows the subject in a clause or sentence: i.e. the verb; the verb + the object; the verb + the complement; etc.

predicative (p. 96) (of an adjective) coming after a copular verb such as *be*, *become*, *feel*, etc.: e.g. *cold* in *the weather was cold*, or *unhappy* in *Paul looks unhappy*. Compare **attributive**, **postpositive**.

prefix (p. 69; p. 105; p. 168) a fixed group of letters that you add at the beginning of a word to form another word, usually with a different but related meaning: e.g. *un-* in *unhappiness*; *dis-* in *disobedient*; *de-* in *decontaminate*. Compare **suffix**.

premodifier (p. 84; p. 108) in a noun phrase or adjective phrase, a word that comes before the noun or adjective and tells you more about it: e.g. *old* in *the old wardrobe*, or *extremely* in *extremely complex*. Compare **postmodifier**.

preposition (p. 186) a word or phrase that links two parts of a clause or sentence, showing a relationship of space, time, cause, manner or means, etc.: e.g. *over* in *I climbed over the fence*, or *from* in *ten miles from where we live*.

prepositional complement (p. 186) the words that follow a preposition: e.g. *the fence* in *I climbed over the fence*, or *where we live* in *ten miles from where we live*.

prepositional phrase (p. 186) a preposition followed by a prepositional complement: e.g. *over the fence* in *I climbed over the fence*, or *from where we live* in *ten miles from where we live*.

prepositional verb (p. 153) a **multi-word verb** that has a preposition as its particle: e.g. *look after*, meaning 'take care of'.

present participle (p. 145) the **-ing form** of a verb used with *be* to express present, future, or past time, etc.: e.g. *wearing* in *he is wearing a blue jumper*, or *eating* in *she was eating an apple*.

present perfect (p. 164) the **aspect** of a verb that consists of the verb *have* in the present tense (i.e. *has/have*) followed by a past participle: e.g. *has worked*, *have seen*. Compare **past perfect**.

present progressive (p. 165) the **aspect** of a verb that consists of the verb *be* in the present tense (i.e. *am/is/are*) followed by a present participle: e.g. *is working*, *are seeing*. Compare **past progressive**.

present tense (p. 160) see **simple present tense**.

primary verb (p. 146) a verb that you can use as a main verb or as an auxiliary verb: i.e. *be*, *have*, *do*. Compare **modal verb**.

pro-form (p. 212) a word that you use in place of a longer word or phrase, usually to avoid repetition: e.g. *it* in *he closed the door and locked it*, or *did* in *Ben worked harder than Sue did*.

progressive aspect (p. 165) the **aspect** of a verb that consists of the verb *be* followed by a present participle: e.g. *is working*, *were seeing*. See also **past progressive**, **present progressive**.

pronoun (p. 112) a word that is used to replace a noun or noun phrase: e.g. *you*, *it*, *herself*, *mine*, *this* (in *this is* . . .), *who*, *each other*, *everything*, *both* (in *both are* . . .), *none*.

proper noun (p. 50) a noun that names a specific person, place, etc., and is written with an initial capital letter: e.g. *Jack*, *Quebec*, *January*, *Buddhism*. Compare **common noun**.

reciprocal pronoun (p. 123) either of the phrases *each other* or *one another*, used to show a mutual or two-way action or relationship.

reflexive pronoun (p. 116) any of the pronouns *myself, yourself, himself, herself, itself, oneself, ourselves, yourselves*, or *themselves*.

reflexive verb (p. 151) a verb whose direct object is a reflexive pronoun: e.g. *they absented themselves, I pride myself*.

regular (p. 56; p. 135) that follows the usual pattern for words of its class or type: e.g. *books* is a regular plural form; *play* is a regular verb. Compare **irregular**.

relative adverb (p. 122) either of the adverbs *when* or *where* used at the beginning of a relative clause.

relative clause (p. 88) a clause beginning with *that, which, who, whom, whose, when*, or *where* that usually tells you more about the noun it follows: e.g. *who live here* in *the people who live here*, or *in which it was wrapped* in *the paper in which it was wrapped*. See also **non-restrictive**, **restrictive**, **sentential relative clause**.

relative pronoun (p. 122) any of the pronouns *that, which, who, whom*, or *whose* used at the beginning of a relative clause.

reported clause (p. 221) in a sentence containing direct or indirect speech, the clause that tells you what was said: e.g. *'I'm not sure'* in *Mandy said, 'I'm not sure'*, or *that it didn't matter* in *Pete replied that it didn't matter*.

reported speech = **indirect speech**.

reporting clause (p. 220) in a sentence containing direct or indirect speech, the clause that contains the verb of speaking and its subject: e.g. *Mandy said* in *Mandy said, 'I'm not sure'*, or *Pete replied* in *Pete replied that it didn't matter*.

restrictive (p. 88; p. 93) (of a relative clause, noun phrase in apposition, etc.) containing essential information that cannot be removed without making the meaning unclear: e.g. *that needs repairing* in *The computer that needs repairing is over there*. Compare **non-restrictive**.

rhetorical question (p. 39) a question to which a reply is not expected: e.g. *Who knows?*

second person (p. 114) being the person or people you are talking to: e.g. the second person pronouns *you, yourself, yourselves*, etc.

sentence (p. 28) a meaningful string of words, usually with a capital letter at the beginning and a full stop, question mark, or exclamation mark at the end. See also **complex sentence, compound sentence, major sentence, minor sentence, multiple sentence, simple sentence**.

sentential relative clause (p. 90) a relative clause that refers back to a whole clause: e.g. *which was not surprising* in *He failed the exam, which was not surprising*.

-s form (p. 136) the form of a verb used in the third person singular of the present tense, usually consisting of the **base form** plus the ending -s: e.g. *looks, comes, breaks, tries*.

simple adverb (p. 172) an adverb that consists of a single word, such as *up, out, here, too, very, often*. Compare **compound adverb**.

simple past tense (p. 161) the -ed form (or irregular equivalent) of a verb, chiefly used to refer to past time: e.g. *opened* in *I opened the door* or *was* in *she was angry*.

simple preposition (p. 188) a preposition that consists of a single word, such as *on, off, with, for, to, at*. Compare complex preposition.

simple present tense (p. 160) the base form and -s form of a verb, chiefly used to refer to present time: e.g. *live* in *I live in Kent*, or *rains* in *it always rains at the weekend*.

simple sentence (p. 29) a sentence that contains a single clause, and that cannot be broken into two or more sentences: e.g. *The soup is cold*. Compare **multiple sentence**.

singular (p. 56) referring to one person, thing, etc.: e.g. *hat* is a singular noun; *this* is a singular pronoun; *has* is a singular verb. Compare **plural**.

split infinitive (p. 174) an infinitive with an adverb between *to* and the main part of the verb: e.g. *to boldly go*.

standard English (p. 20) the form of English that most educated people regard as correct and acceptable.

stress (p. 229) saying a word (or part of a word) more loudly to draw attention to it.

subject (p. 30) the word or phrase – often a noun or pronoun – that usually comes before the verb: e.g. *the girl* in *the girl kicked the ball*. Compare **object**.

subject complement (p. 34) a **complement** that provides information about the subject of a verb: e.g. *cold* in *the tea is cold*. Compare **object complement**.

subjective (p. 129) (referring to) the case or form of pronoun when it is used as the subject of a verb: e.g. *I, he, she, we, they, who*. Compare **objective**.

subjunct (p. 181) an adverbial that has a subordinate role: e.g. *please* in *Could you close the door, please?* or *really* in *He sounded really unhappy*. Compare **adjunct, conjunct, disjunct**.

subjunctive mood (p. 156) the way a verb is used to express a demand, a wish, a possibility, etc.: e.g. *leave* in *she insisted that he leave at once*, or *were* in *if I were prime minister*. Compare **imperative mood, indicative mood**.

subordinate clause (p. 29; p. 202; p. 206) a clause that sounds incomplete and that cannot stand alone as a sentence, e.g. *if it rains* in the sentence *If it rains we can go to the cinema.* Compare **main clause**.

subordinating conjunction (p. 197) a conjunction that links parts of a sentence that do not have the same status: e.g. *when* in *we left when it began to rain.* Compare **coordinating conjunction**.

subordination (p. 206) the relationship or linking of parts of a sentence that do not have the same status, usually with a subordinating conjunction. Compare **coordination**.

subordinator = **subordinating conjunction**.

suffix (p. 68; p. 104; p. 168) a fixed ending that you add to a word (or to part of a word) to form a new word: e.g. *-ness* in *brightness*; *-able* in *drinkable*; *-ize* in *fossilize*. Compare **prefix**.

superlative (p. 100; p. 173) (of the form of an adjective or adverb) used to compare three or more things, people, events, etc.: e.g. *richest*, *most reliable*, *most urgently*. Compare **comparative**.

syntax (p. 19) the study of the structure of sentences.

tag question (p. 39) a statement followed by a 'tag' such as *is it?*, *don't you?*, etc.: e.g. *It isn't raining, is it?* or *You still love me, don't you?*

tense (p. 160) the form of a verb that tells you what time it refers to. See also **simple past tense**, **simple present tense**.

third person (p. 114) being the person, people, or thing(s) you are talking about: e.g. the third person pronouns *he, him, himself, she, her, herself, it, itself, they, them, themselves,* etc.

transitive (p. 154) (of a verb) used with a direct object: e.g. *hate* in *I hate spiders*, or *made* in *she made a mistake*. Compare **intransitive**. See also **ditransitive**.

uncountable noun (p. 52) a noun that cannot be made plural: e.g. *mud, granite, impatience, knowledge.* Compare **countable noun**.

uncount noun = **uncountable noun**.

variable noun (p. 60) a noun that has different forms in the singular and plural: e.g. *car/cars; foot/feet.* Compare **invariable noun**, **zero plural**.

verb (p. 134) a word that expresses action, change, being, having, etc.: e.g. *run, eat, operate, think, be, have.*

verbless clause (p. 98) a clause in which the verb is omitted: e.g. *if possible; when available.*

verb phrase (p. 134) the verb element of a clause or sentence, consisting of one or more words: e.g. *walked* in *they walked across the field*, or *were walking* in *they were walking across the field*.

vocative (p. 44) a word or phrase that makes it clear who you are talking to: e.g. *waiter* in *Waiter, there's a fly in my soup!*

voice (p. 158) see **active voice**, **passive voice**.

***wh*-word** (p. 120) any of the set of words *how, what, when, where, which, who, whom, whose, why*, etc., used to ask questions or to introduce relative clauses.

word class (p. 22) a category of words that are used for the same purpose or in the same way. The word classes include nouns, adjectives, verbs, etc.

zero article (p. 81) the use of a noun without *a*, *an*, or *the*: e.g. *money* in *money makes the world go round*, or *school* in *go to school*.

zero plural (p. 60) a noun that has the same form in the singular and plural: e.g. *aircraft, deer, series*. Compare **invariable noun**, **variable noun**.

Why grammar?

What is grammar?

Grammar is the study of how a language works. It shows us how the words of a language are put together to make meaningful sentences. It also provides us with names for different types of word or phrase and the tasks they perform in a sentence.

Some people think we are born with a sense of grammar. (The American linguist Noam Chomsky, an authority on the subject, claimed that 'Each person has programmed into his genes a faculty called universal grammar.') Others think we learn it in the same way as we learn the vocabulary of our native language, by imitating others and by being corrected when we make a mistake.

This book deals with the grammar of the English language. If you learn a foreign language, you will find that the conventions of English grammar are not always the same as those of French, German, Latin, etc. However, a knowledge of English grammar will provide you with a useful set of tools for dismantling the grammar of a foreign language and learning how to put it back together again.

The teaching of grammar

Until the middle of the twentieth century, English grammar was taught in British schools in a very formal way. Pupils would learn how to analyse sentences, breaking them down into clauses and word classes, an exercise called *parsing*.

Educational theorists thought that this way of learning about the English language destroyed creativity, and in the 1960s the formal teaching of English grammar in British schools became unfashionable. As a result, many people left school in the 1970s and 1980s with only a hazy knowledge of the conventions of grammar. Those people are the parents and teachers of today's children.

In recent years the pendulum has swung back, and the National Curriculum has brought the teaching of grammar back into the classroom. Pupils at junior school should be 'given opportunities to develop their understanding of the grammar of complex sentences, including clauses and phrases, and taught the standard written forms of nouns, pronouns, verbs, adjectives, adverbs, prepositions, conjunctions and verb tenses'.

As attitudes to the teaching of grammar have changed over the years, so has the grammar that is taught. Traditional grammar was based on the grammar of Latin, and examples were taken from the speeches of great orators or the literary texts of great writers. To many students, this seemed to bear little relation to everyday spoken or written language. Modern grammar has a broader approach, taking in spoken English and the many different varieties of written English – the language of business, journalism, technology, etc., as well as that of literature.

The branches of grammar

Grammar may be divided into two main branches, morphology and syntax.

Morphology deals with the structure of words, including inflection and derivation. **Inflection** is the way words change to show differences of tense (*play/played*), number (*has/have, car/cars*), person (*I/you, am/is/are*), gender (*he/she*), case (*who/whom, Jane/Jane's*), comparison (*small/smaller/smallest*), etc. **Derivation** is the way new words are formed by adding prefixes (*happy/unhappy*), suffixes (*break/breakable*), etc.

Syntax deals with the structure of sentences. This includes the order and arrangement of words within a phrase or clause, and of phrases or clauses within a sentence.

A number of other branches of the study of language are closely related to grammar. These include **semantics** (the study of meaning), **pragmatics** (the study of language in use), and **phonetics** (the study of speech sounds).

GRAMMAR – WHO NEEDS IT?

While correcting the proofs of his last parliamentary speech, the British statesman Benjamin Disraeli said, 'I will not go down to posterity talking bad grammar.'

Others share his opinion on the importance of grammar:

Grammar is the logic of speech, even as logic is the grammar of reason. (Richard Chevenix Trench, *On the Study of Words*)

Like everything metaphysical the harmony between thought and reality is to be found in the grammar of the language. (Ludwig Wittgenstein, *Zettel*)

Grammar, which can govern even kings. (Molière, *Les Femmes savantes*)

The Holy Roman Emperor Sigismund, however, is alleged to have held a different view:

I am the Roman Emperor, and am above grammar.

And the American humorist Artemus Ward, in *Pyrotechny*, asked:

Why care for grammar as long as we are good?

Right or wrong?

There are many different types of English, each appropriate to a different set of circumstances. In a conversation with a friend, you do not use the same form of English as in a letter to your bank manager. What is 'right' in one situation may be 'wrong' in another.

Similarly, different regions of Britain have their own dialects, and different parts of the English-speaking world have their own varieties of English. What is 'right' in one dialect or variety of English may be 'wrong' in standard English.

What is standard English?

Standard English is is the form of English that most educated people regard as correct and acceptable. The grammatical structures described in this book are generally those of standard English (as used in Britain).

Regional dialects of English

A dialect is the form of English spoken by a particular group of people, usually in a particular region of the country. A dialect may have its own word for something, such as

clout (= cloth)   *emmet* (= ant)
mardy (= sulky)   *happen* (= perhaps)

A dialect may also have different ways of putting words together, such as

I be Sally's brother. (= I am Sally's brother.)
He were waiting outside. (= He was waiting outside.)
We was on our way home. (= We were on our way home.)

Do not confuse accent with dialect. Accent relates only to the way words are pronounced, not the form or meaning of the words. Many people speak standard English with a regional accent.

International varieties of English

English is the native language of people in many parts of the world: Britain, the USA, Canada, Australia, New Zealand, some countries of Africa and Asia, and some islands of the Caribbean. The form of English used in each of these nations has its own peculiarities.

For example, if you ask a British person if they have a pen, the answer is likely to be 'Yes, I have' or 'No, I haven't'. If you ask an American the same question, the answer is likely to be 'Yes, I do' or 'No, I don't'.

Different English-speaking countries also have differences of vocabulary:

- in American English, *faucet* means 'tap', *sidewalk* means 'pavement', etc.
- in Australian English, *chook* means 'chicken', *fossick* means 'search', etc.

Speech and writing

Most people, however well educated, do not speak in perfectly constructed standard English sentences, unless they are reading a prepared speech. Spoken language differs from written language in several ways:

- when you speak, you often give visual clues that replace spoken words. You may point to something as you say 'Whose is this?'.

- when you write, you usually have time to think about sentence structure and vocabulary.

- when you speak, you can vary the sound of your voice to add meaning to what you say. You can use intonation to make a statement sound like a question, or to express surprise, sarcasm, anger, etc.

- when you write, you can use punctuation and other devices (such as paragraphs and page layout) to make your meaning clear.

Grammar and usage

Grammar is the way language is put together, and usage is the way people actually use it. You cannot study grammar without taking usage into account, and vice versa. There are a number of issues of usage that are guaranteed to raise the hackles of a certain sector of the population. These grammatical hot potatoes include the following 'seven deadly sins':

- splitting the infinitive
- ending a sentence with a preposition
- starting a sentence with *and* or *but*
- saying *who* instead of *whom*
- using *I will* when you mean *I shall*
- saying *different to* instead of *different from*
- using *hopefully* when you mean *it is hoped that*

In many such cases, there is no right or wrong. There are times when avoiding a split infinitive can lead to ambiguity. In informal speech, saying *the woman I spoke to* is far more natural than saying *the woman to whom I spoke*. And in modern English, the difference between *I will* and *I shall* has all but disappeared.

Word classes

A **word class**, also called a **part of speech**, is a category of words that are used for the same purpose or in the same way. The eight principal word classes described in this book are:

- nouns, e.g. *car, boy, Sarah, happiness.*
- determiners, e.g. *a, the, this, many.*
- adjectives, e.g. *wet, green, Australian, breakable.*
- pronouns, e.g. *we, it, something, anybody.*
- verbs, e.g. *be, do, operate, think.*
- adverbs, e.g. *slowly, obviously, well, very.*
- prepositions, e.g. *to, over, behind, after.*
- conjunctions, e.g. *and, or, while, if.*

(Some grammars and dictionaries also treat interjections (e.g. *ah, ouch, wow*) as a word class. You will find more information about these on page 42.)

Nouns

Nouns are words for things, feelings, people, places, etc., e.g. *house, dog, patience, father-in-law, Jane, airport, Paris.*

There are various types of noun: proper nouns and common nouns; countable nouns and uncountable nouns; concrete nouns and abstract nouns; etc.

You will find more information about all these types of noun on pages 48–55.

Determiners

Determiners are words like *a, the, my, this, some,* or *many.* They come before a noun and tell you how much, how many, which, whose, etc. There are several groups of determiners:

- articles, i.e. *a, an, the.*
- possessives, i.e. *my, your, his, her, its, one's, our, their.*
- demonstratives, i.e. *this, that, these, those.*
- interrogatives, i.e. *what, which, whose.*
- numerals, e.g. *one, two, three, four; first, second, third, fourth.*
- fractions and multipliers, e.g. *half, three-quarters, double, twice.*
- quantifiers, e.g. *all, each, both, some, any, no, several.*

You will find more information about determiners on pages 76–83.

Adjectives

Adjectives are words that tell you more about a noun, e.g. *good, young, black, interesting, German, wooden*. They tell you what someone or something is like, where someone is from, what something is made of, etc.

There are various types of adjective: attributive adjectives and predicative adjectives; central adjectives and peripheral adjectives; gradable adjectives and non-gradable adjectives; etc.

You will find more information about all these types of adjective on pages 96–109.

Pronouns

Pronouns are words that you use instead of nouns, often to avoid repetition. There are a number of different types of pronoun:

- personal pronouns, e.g. *I, me, you, him, she, her, it, us, they.*
- reflexive pronouns, e.g. *myself, itself, ourselves, yourselves.*
- possessives, e.g. *my, mine, your, yours, his, her, hers, their, theirs.*
- demonstratives, e.g. *this, that, these, those.*
- interrogatives, e.g. *what, which, who, whom, whose.*
- relative pronouns, e.g. *that, which, who, whom, whose.*
- reciprocal pronouns, e.g. *each other, one another.*
- indefinite pronouns, e.g. *everything, nobody, all, both, either, another.*

You will find more information about pronouns on pages 112–31.

Verbs

Verbs are words that express action, movement, change, being, having, etc., e.g. *walk, drink, use, consider, melt, be, remain, have, seem.*

There are various types of verb: main verbs and auxiliary verbs; regular verbs and irregular verbs; transitive verbs and intransitive verbs; etc.

You will find more information about all these types of verb on pages 134–55.

Adverbs

Adverbs are words that tell you when, where, how, why, etc., e.g. *today, never, there, quickly, fortunately.* They may tell you more about a verb, an adjective, another adverb, or a whole sentence.

You will find more information about adverbs on pages 172–83.

{CONTD}

Prepositions

Prepositions are words or phrases that link two parts of a sentence (often a verb and a noun phrase), e.g. *over, out of, before, during, in spite of*.

You will find more information about prepositions on pages 186–93.

Conjunctions

Conjunctions are words or phrases that link two clauses or other parts of a sentence. There are two types of conjunction:

- coordinating conjunctions, e.g. *and, or, but*.
- subordinating conjunctions, e.g. *when, while, if, although, because*.

You will find more information about conjunctions on pages 196–9.

Words that belong to more than one word class

Many words belong to more than one word class. Words like *work, play, drive, run, walk, jump*, etc., are nouns and verbs:

*I usually cycle to **work**.*	*I **work** in a factory.*
*The horse fell at the first **jump**.*	*The horse **jumped** over the fence.*

Words like *cold, square, silver*, etc., are nouns and adjectives:

*a **square** of carpet*	*a **square** box*
*a ring made of **silver***	***silver** paint*

Words like *in, above, off*, etc., are adverbs and prepositions:

*He opened the door and went **in**.*	*She lives **in** a bungalow.*
*I took my shoes **off**.*	*Take your feet **off** that chair!*

Words like *until, after, before*, etc., are prepositions and conjunctions:

*We'll wait **until** midnight.*	*We'll wait **until** it stops raining.*
*They left **before** dawn.*	*They left **before** you arrived.*

The word *round* belongs to no fewer than five word classes:

*a **round** of drinks* (noun)	*Wind the tape **round** the spool.*
*A circle is **round**.* (adjective)	(preposition)
*Summer will soon come **round** again.* (adverb)	*as we **rounded** the bend* (verb)

Conversion

Many 'new' nouns, verbs, etc., are coined by adopting words from different word classes. This process is called **conversion**. Here are just a few examples:

- verb → noun

  a *laugh*, a *stop*, a *must*, a *find*, an *offer*

- adjective → noun

  a *regular*, a *natural*, a *final*, a *comic*, a *daily*

- noun → verb

  to *rubbish*, to *ship*, to *fax*, to *finance*, to *microwave*

- adjective → verb

  to *faint*, to *slim*, to *tidy*, to *calm*, to *soundproof*

RHYME AND REASON

The following rhyme – which exists in many variant forms – was once used to help schoolchildren learn about word classes (or parts of speech):

Every name is called a **noun**,
As *field* and *fountain*, *street* and *town*;
In place of noun the **pronoun** stands,
As *he* and *she* can clap their hands;
The **adjective** describes a thing,
As *magic* wand or *bridal* ring;
The **verb** means action, something done –
To *read* and *write*, to *jump* and *run*;
How things are done, the **adverbs** tell,
As *quickly*, *slowly*, *badly*, *well*;
The **preposition** shows relation,
As *in* the street or *at* the station;
Conjunctions join, in many ways,
Sentences, words, *or* phrase *and* phrase;
The **interjection** cries out, *'Hark!*
I need an exclamation mark!'

Sentences – the basics

What is a sentence?

A **sentence** is a string of words with a capital letter at the beginning and a full stop (or a question mark or an exclamation mark) at the end. The following examples are all sentences:

She left in a taxi.   *Is it raining?*
I opened the door.   *Go away!*

A sentence must also make sense and sound complete. The following examples are *not* sentences:

*A taxi left she.   **In a taxi.*

Major sentences and minor sentences

There are two types of sentence: major sentences and minor sentences. A **major sentence** must contain a verb. It may be:

- a statement: *I opened the door.*; *She left in a taxi.*
- a question: *Is it raining?*; *Where do you live?*
- a command, instruction, or request: *Go away!*; *Unscrew the lid.*; *Close the door, please.*
- an exclamation: *What a strange noise that was!*; *Isn't it infuriating!*

A major sentence must also sound complete. Compare the following examples:

I opened the door.   **When I opened the door.*

Both have a capital letter, a verb, and a full stop, but the second example sounds incomplete – you want to know what happened when I opened the door.

A **minor sentence** does not have to contain a verb, but it must still make sense and sound complete. Minor sentences include:

- exclamations and interjections: *What a pity!*; *All aboard!*; *Hi!*; *Ouch!*
- formulaic expressions: *Good morning!*; *Pleased to meet you.*
- shortened forms of questions: *Coffee?* (= *Would you like a cup of coffee?*); *Having trouble?* (= *Are you having trouble?*)
- signs, notices, etc.: *No parking*; *For sale*; *Way out*; *Boats for hire*
- instructions, messages, etc.: *Handle with care.*; *Wish you were here!*
- sayings: *In for a penny, in for a pound.*

What is a clause?

A **clause** is a part of a sentence. Most clauses contain a verb. Both the following sentences are made up of two clauses:

Pete cooked the dinner | while Anne had a bath.
If it rains | we can go to the cinema.

There are two types of clause: main clauses and subordinate clauses. A **main clause** is like a sentence – it sounds complete:

Pete cooked the dinner   *we can go to the cinema*

A **subordinate clause** cannot stand alone as a sentence – it sounds incomplete. A subordinate clause often begins with a word like *when, if,* etc.:

while Anne had a bath   *if it rains*

Simple sentences and multiple sentences

Major sentences can be divided into two groups: simple sentences and multiple sentences. A **simple sentence** contains a single clause:

The cat ran across the road.   *We left.*

A **multiple sentence** contains more than one clause:

The cat ran across the road and the dog chased it.
We left when the show was over.

The first example contains two main clauses (*the cat ran across the road* and *the dog chased it*). The second contains a main clause (*we left*) and a subordinate clause (*when the show was over*).

Compound sentences and complex sentences

Multiple sentences can be further subdivided into two groups: compound sentences and complex sentences. A **compound sentence** contains two main clauses linked by *and, or, but,* etc.: *The cat ran across the road and the dog chased it.*

A **complex sentence** contains a main clause and a subordinate clause beginning with *while, when, before, after, if, because,* etc.: *We left when the show was over.*

You will find more information about sentences and clauses in the section 'Sentence structure' beginning on page 202.

The parts of a clause

Every clause or sentence is made up of a number of different parts or elements. Each of these parts may be a single word or a group of words. They include:

- the subject, e.g. *Pete* in *Pete cooked the dinner.*
- the verb, e.g. *cooked* in *Pete cooked the dinner.*
- the object, e.g. *the dinner* in *Pete cooked the dinner.*
- the complement, e.g. *angry* in *I was angry.*
- the adverbial, e.g. *over the fence* in *The horse jumped over the fence.*

Few clauses or sentences contain all these elements, but most contain a subject and verb.

The subject

The **subject** of a clause or sentence is usually a noun or pronoun. (In all the examples that follow, the subject is the word or words in bold type.) It may be:

- a common noun: *Mice like cheese.*
- a proper noun: *Beth likes cheese.*
- a pronoun: *I like cheese.*

It may also be a phrase containing one or more nouns or pronouns:

My dog likes cheese. **The old man in the armchair** likes cheese.
Kate, Sam, and Jack like cheese.
She and I like cheese.

There is only one subject – in *she and I like cheese*, the phrase *she and I* is a single plural subject, not two separate subjects. Note also that when a pronoun is the subject it is in the subjective form *I, he, she, we,* or *they* (not the objective form *me, him, her, us,* or *them*).

Other types of subject include *-ing* forms of verbs:

Smoking is forbidden. **Learning a foreign language** takes time.
Driving fast uses more fuel.

Sometimes the subject may itself be a clause:

What you wear doesn't matter. **How the lion escaped** remains a mystery.
That he still loved her was obvious.

The position of the subject

The subject usually comes at the beginning of the clause or sentence, before the verb. Exceptions include:

- questions

  *Is **Mary** here?*   *Are **they** pleased?*

- sentences or clauses where the normal pattern is changed for emphasis or effect

  *In came **her father**.*   *There goes **my pay rise!***

- clauses introduced by *hardly, scarcely, no sooner,* etc.

  *No sooner had **she** posted the letter, . . .*

- direct speech

  *'Where?' asked **the child**.*   *'Over there,' **I** replied.*

- commands and similar sentences that use a verb without a subject

  Come in!   *Open the window.*

Whatever its position, the subject is the person, thing, situation, etc. that governs the form of the verb, and the ending of the verb may change according to whether the subject is singular, plural, etc.:

*Mice **like** cheese.*   ***Is** Mary here?*
*My dog **likes** cheese.*   ***Are** they pleased?*

You will find more information about these changes in verb ending in the section 'Concord' on page 36.

THERE IS SAFETY IN NUMBERS

The word *there* often takes the place of the subject before the verb:

There's no business like show business.   *There are plenty more fish in the sea.*
There seems to be a problem.   *There seem to be no biscuits left.*

However, it is what follows the verb that determines whether you use *is* or *are, seems* or *seem,* etc.: *plenty more fish* is plural, so you use *are; a problem* is singular, so you use *seems.*

{CONTD}

The object

There are two types of object: the **direct object** (DO) and the **indirect object** (IO). Both are affected, directly or indirectly, by the action of the verb, and the difference between them is best illustrated by example. In the following four sentences, *a present* is the direct object and *the child* is the indirect object:

I gave the child a present.   *I gave a present to the child.*
I bought the child a present.   *I bought a present for the child.*

Like the subject, the object may be:

- a common noun

*I like **cats**.* (DO)   *He gives **people** money.* (IO)

- a proper noun

*I like **London**.* (DO)   *They gave **Jane** a book.* (IO)

- a pronoun

*I like **him**.* (DO)   *We gave **them** a warning.* (IO)

Note that when a pronoun is the object of a clause it is in the objective form *me, him, her, us*, or *them* (not the subjective form *I, he, she, we, they*).

- a phrase containing one or more nouns or pronouns

*I like **your house**.* (DO)   *She gave **the boy** a kick.* (IO)
*I like **rock, jazz, and classical**   *I'll give **the walls, door, and*
***music**.* (DO)   ***ceiling** a coat of paint.* (IO)
*I like **those red flowers behind**   *He gave **the old man in the*
***the tree**.* (DO)   ***armchair** a cup of tea.* (IO)

- an *-ing* form

*I like **dancing**.* (DO)   *I'll give **dieting** a try.* (IO)

- a clause

*She repeated **what he said**.* (DO)   *They explained **how it worked**.*
          (DO)

*I noticed **that the window was**   *I'll give **what you told me** some*
***broken**.* (DO)   *thought.* (IO)

The position of the object

Both the direct object and the indirect object usually follow the verb. If the indirect object is not preceded by *to*, *for*, etc., it usually comes before the direct object:

*He threw **the dog a bone**.* (IO DO)   *She told **me a lie**.* (IO DO)

However, the direct object may occasionally come before the indirect object:

*I gave **you it** yesterday.* (IO DO) or *I gave **it you** yesterday.* (DO IO)

An indirect object is usually found in clauses that also have a direct object. However, the indirect object can sometimes stand alone, taking the place of the direct object, as in:

*I paid **my accountant**.* (IO)   *She told **her friend**.* (IO)
compare *I paid **my accountant her***   compare *She told **her friend***
  fee. (IO DO)   ***what had happened**.* (IO DO)

The complement

The word or phrase that follows verbs like *be*, *become*, *feel*, etc., is called the **complement**. Verbs that have a complement instead of (or as well as) an object are called copular or linking verbs. The complement provides further information about the subject or object of the verb:

Anna is my niece. (subject + copular verb + complement)
Anna hates my niece. (subject + transitive verb + direct object)

The complement is usually an adjective or noun phrase:

*Our dog is **a poodle**.*   *The tea is **cold**.*
*The caterpillar became **a butterfly**.*   *The weather became **stormy**.*
*I feel **a fool**.*   *He felt **ill**.*
*She remained **my friend**.*   *The seat remained **unoccupied**.*

Here are some more examples with different copular verbs:

*Jonathan **seems** rather worried.*   *The project **sounds** very interesting.*
*It **appears** impossible.*   *That soup **smells** appetizing!*
*The room **grew** colder.*   *The apple **tasted** sour.*
*The liquid **will turn** blue.*

The complement may also be a pronoun or a clause:

*That is **it**.*   *This is **what I'm looking for**.*

{CONTD}

Subject complements and object complements

A **subject complement** provides further information about the subject of the verb:

Our dog is **a poodle**.　　　　　*Jonathan* seems **rather worried**.
The weather became **stormy**.　　*The project* sounds **very**
　　　　　　　　　　　　　　　　　　　　interesting.
She remained **my friend**.

Some copular verbs can have an object *and* a complement. In such cases the complement is an **object complement** – it provides further information about the object of the verb. In the following example, *her hair* is the direct object of the verb and *green* is the object complement:

*The shampoo turned **her hair green**.*

Here are some more examples:

*The students found **this question**　*These modifications will make **the**
　very difficult.　　　　　　　　　　　**car safer**.
*You'll make **him a laughing-stock**.　*They appointed **me chairman**.

A subject complement usually follows the verb. An object complement usually follows the direct object to which it relates.

The adverbial

The **adverbial** is a word or phrase that provides further information, usually about the verb. It may be:

- an adverb

  *She left **suddenly**.*　　　　　　*It was raining **heavily**.*

- a phrase containing one or more adverbs

  *She left **very soon afterwards**.*　*He played **remarkably well**.*

- a phrase beginning with a preposition

  *She left **in a taxi**.*　　　　　　　*The horse jumped **over the fence**.*
  *Put your shoes **under the bed**.*　*He was **on his own**.*

- a noun phrase

  *She left **this morning**.*　　　　　*He died **last June**.*

- a subordinate clause

  *She left **when she heard the news**.*　*He stopped **because he was tired**.*

The position of the adverbial

The adverbial is usually found at the end of the clause, but it can sometimes be placed before or after the subject:

***Little by little** he opened the door.   He **suddenly** opened the door.*

There may be more than one adverbial in a single clause or sentence:

*She left **very soon afterwards in a taxi**.*
*She left **suddenly this morning when she heard the news**.*

Not every clause needs an adverbial, but some verbs are grammatically
incomplete without one:

*She put the money **in her purse**.   Please keep **off the grass**.*
*A leather jacket lay **on the bed**.   He leaned **against the wall**.*

You will find further information about adverbials in the section 'Adverbs'
beginning on page 172.

Clause patterns

The five basic elements of the clause – subject (S), verb (V), object (O),
complement (C), and adverbial (A) – are most frequently arranged in one
of the following patterns:

The doctor left. **S** (the doctor) + **V** (left)
The doctor crossed the road. **S** (the doctor) + **V** (crossed) + **O** (the road)
The doctor is short-sighted. **S** (the doctor) + **V** (is) + **C** (short-sighted)
The doctor works at the hospital. **S** (the doctor) + **V** (works) + **A** (at the
     hospital)
The doctor gave me a prescription. **S** (the doctor) + **V** (gave) + **O** (me) + **O**
     (a prescription)
The doctor makes his patients well. **S** (the doctor) + **V** (makes) + **O** (his
     patients) + **C** (well)
The doctor has driven his car into a tree. **S** (the doctor) + **V** (has driven) +
     O (his car) + **A** (into a tree)

In sentences of this type, everything that follows the subject (V; V + O; V
+ A; V + O + C; etc.) is called the **predicate**.

Many other combinations of the basic elements S, V, O, A, C, are possible:

She is never happy. (S V A C)   *Is Mary here?* (V S A)
He looked out of the window again.   *Are they pleased?* (V S C)
     (S V A A)   *'Where?' asked the child.* (O V S)
Come in! (V A)   *'Over there,' I replied.* (O S V)
Open the door. (V O)   *There goes my pay rise!* (A V S)
Give him the book. (V O O)   *Off they went.* (A S V)

Concord

When you change the subject of a verb from singular to plural, you sometimes have to change the verb as well:

The boy ***has*** *a dog.* (singular subject + singular verb)
The boys ***have*** *a dog.* (plural subject + plural verb)

This is called **concord** (or **agreement**). In the first sentence the verb *has* agrees with the singular subject (*the boy*). In the second sentence, when the subject becomes plural (*the boys*), the verb must change to *have* to remain in concord.

Concord usually occurs between the subject and verb of a clause or sentence. It never occurs between the verb and its object. In the following two sentences, when the singular object (*a dog*) becomes plural (*several dogs*) the verb does not change:

The boy ***has*** *a dog.*   *The boy* ***has*** *several dogs.*

In English many verbs have a different form only in the third person singular (i.e. the form used with *he*, *she*, or *it*) of the present tense. In other persons of the present tense and in other tenses the verb does not change:

I ***have*** *a dog.* (first person singular, present tense)
We ***have*** *a dog.* (first person plural, present tense)

The boy ***had*** *a dog.* (third person singular, past tense)
The boys ***had*** *a dog.* (third person plural, past tense)

The verb *be*, however, has different forms for the first and third persons singular of the present and past tenses:

I ***am*** *cold. / We* ***are*** *cold.*   *I* ***was*** *warm. / We* ***were*** *warm.*
She ***is*** *cold. / They* ***are*** *cold.*   *He* ***was*** *warm. / They* ***were*** *warm.*

Concord also occurs

- between the subject and object of reflexive verbs:

  I *kicked* ***myself***.   ***The children*** *washed* ***themselves***.

- between the subject and a possessive that comes before the object:

  He *opened* ***his*** *bag.*   ***We*** *offered* ***our*** *apologies.*

- between the subject and the subject complement, when the complement is a noun or pronoun:

  She is **a doctor**. / **They** are **doctors**.
  This is a **more expensive one**. / **These** are **more expensive ones**.

- between the object and the object complement, when the complement is a noun or pronoun:

  They made **him an honorary member**. / He made **them honorary members**.

This is **grammatical concord**. But the verb can agree with the meaning of the subject rather than its grammatical form (this is called **notional concord**): Fifty pounds **is** [not *****are**] not enough.

Sometimes the verb agrees with the part of the subject that is closest to it (**proximity concord**). This is usually considered grammatically incorrect, as in: *****A box of chocolates **were** given to the winner.

However, proximity concord may sometimes be acceptable, as in the following example: A number of people **have** telephoned.

THOU SHALT NOT STEAL

In earlier times, the second person singular of the verb had a different form from the second person plural. It also had a different pronoun – *thou* instead of *you*:

thou art / you are	thou wert / you were
thou shalt / you shall	thou wilt / you will
thou hast / you have	thou hadst / you had
thou dost / you do	thou didst / you did
thou goest / you go	thou livest / you live

The third person singular of the present tense also had a different form: *hath* instead of has, *doth* instead of *does*, *saith* instead of *says*, etc.

In some dialects of modern English the *thou* form of the verb (together with related pronouns such as *thee, thy, thine*) is still in everyday use.

Types of sentence

There are four types of sentence: statements, questions, directives (i.e. commands, instructions, or requests), and exclamations.

- a statement usually contains a subject, which comes before the verb: *The children were quiet.*; *She knows the answer.*
- a question usually contains a subject, which comes after (part of) the verb: *Were the children quiet?*; *Does she know the answer?*
- a command, instruction, or request usually does not contain a subject, and the verb is in the imperative mood: *Be quiet!*; *Take care!*
- an exclamation usually has a fixed structure: *How quiet they are!*; *Aren't the children quiet!*

Statements

A **statement** provides information. It usually has a full stop at the end:

The files had been destroyed.   *We drove home in silence.*

The subject occasionally follows the verb in statements:

- for emphasis or effect: *Down came the rain.*
- when a clause begins with *hardly, scarcely, no sooner,* etc.: *No sooner had she posted the letter, . . .*
- in direct speech: *'Thank you,' said Mary.*

Questions

A **question** seeks information. It usually has a question mark at the end:

Is he her son?   *Where's my scarf?*

There are several different types of question: *yes-no* questions, alternative questions, *wh*-questions, rhetorical questions, etc.

yes-no questions

A *yes-no* **question** can be answered by *yes* or *no* alone (although further information may be given in the reply). *Is he her son?* is a *yes-no* question. Possible replies include: *Yes; No; Yes, he is; No, he's her brother.*

A *yes-no* question may be positive or negative:

Did he lock the door?   *Didn't he lock the door?*

A *yes-no* question may also take the form of a statement, with the subject before the verb. Such statements have a question mark at the end to show that you would say the sentence with your voice rising on the last word:

He won?   *They've gone home?*

Alternative questions and *wh*-questions

An **alternative question** cannot be answered by *yes* or *no* alone. The reply must contain one of the words in the question (or a word that covers both options). *Are you left-handed or right-handed?* is an alternative question. Possible replies include: *Left-handed; Right-handed; I'm ambidextrous.*

A ***wh*-question** begins with one of the set of words *how, what, when, where, who, why,* etc. *Where's my scarf?* is a *wh*-question. Possible replies include: *In the drawer; Round your neck; Over there; Where you left it.*

Rhetorical questions

A **rhetorical question** looks and sounds like an ordinary question, but a reply is not expected. You may use a rhetorical question to express resignation, complain, protest, etc. Here are some examples:

*Why does it always rain at the   Is it my fault if he never phones
    weekend?   his mother?*

TAGGING ALONG

A *yes-no* question sometimes consists of a statement followed by a 'tag' such as *is it?, don't you?,* etc. These are called **tag questions**.

It isn't raining, is it?   *You still love me, don't you?*

When you use a tag question, you often expect or hope to receive a particular answer. Compare *You still love me, don't you?* with the straightforward question *Do you still love me?*

With a different tone of voice, you can make a tag question sound like a statement or an exclamation that doesn't need a reply:

He forgot, didn't he?   *She's spent it all, hasn't she?*

A tag question may also be used to

- make a suggestion: *I've lost my boots. – They aren't in the hall, are they?*
- make a polite request: *You couldn't lend me five pounds, could you?*
- express anger, etc.: *I've never had the opportunity, have I?*

{CONTD}

Directives

Commands, instructions, requests, etc., are sometimes known collectively as **directives**. Most directives contain a verb in the imperative mood. The imperative form of the verb is the same as the infinitive, without *to*. You can make it negative by adding *do not* or *don't* before the main verb:

Don't go away!   *Please do not touch the exhibits.*

Sometimes a positive imperative is reinforced by adding *do*, for extra emphasis, politeness, etc.:

Do be quiet!   *Do sit down.*

Commands

A **command** usually has an exclamation mark at the end:

Go away!   *Don't be rude!*

The verb is imperative and there is usually no subject. You may, however, add a subject for emphasis or to make it clear who you are talking to:

Nobody look!   *You come here!*

Instructions

An **instruction** also has an imperative verb without a subject. There is usually no exclamation mark:

Screw the bracket to the wall.   *Fry the onions for two minutes.*

On labels or packaging, in recipe books, etc., instructions are often minor sentences in which the object of a verb may be missing:

Serve hot or cold. (= Serve the food, drink, etc., hot or cold)

Requests

A **request** that uses an imperative verb often contains the word *please*, for politeness. More urgent requests may have an exclamation mark:

Close the door, please.   *Help me!*

Polite requests are often phrased as questions:

Will you move your bag, please?   *Could you pass me the salt, please?*

Other types of directive

Other types of directive using imperative verbs include:

- advice and warnings: *Do not exceed the stated dose.*
- invitations: *Come and stay for the weekend.*
- traditional formulae expressing good wishes, etc.: *Enjoy yourself!*

Exclamations

An **exclamation** expresses surprise, pleasure, admiration, anger, indignation, etc. Exclamations always end with an exclamation mark. They are usually major or minor sentences, often beginning with the word *what* or *how*:

What an ugly dog he had!   *How she loved that house!*
What a noise they are making!   *How quiet they are!*

Note that the object or complement is often placed before the subject, rather than after the verb as in a statement:

Statement: *They are quiet.* (subject + verb + complement)
Exclamation: *How quiet they are!* (how + complement + subject + verb)

The structure of an exclamation is also different from that of a question, in which the word *how* has a different meaning:

Question: *How happy is he?*   Exclamation: *How happy he is!*

Exclamations beginning with *what* or *how* are often shortened to the form of a minor sentence:

What fun [we will have]*!*   *How annoying* [it is]*!*

Other exclamations in the form of a minor sentence include words and phrases such as: *For goodness' sake!*; *Oh dear!*; *You lucky thing!*; *Amazing!*

In speech and informal writing there is often a fine dividing line between questions and exclamations:

What have you done to my new car?!   *Who do they think I am!?*

An exclamation may also be phrased as a negative question, but with an exclamation mark at the end:

Isn't it a shame!   *Wasn't it boring!*

Interjections

An **interjection** is an exclamatory sound that you make to show surprise, admiration, triumph, anger, pain, disgust, etc.: *Gosh!, Wow!, Hooray!, Oi!, Ouch!, Yuk!, Ah!, Eh?, Oops!*

Some grammar books (and most dictionaries) regard interjections as a word class, like prepositions or nouns. Others regard them as a type of sentence, like exclamations or questions.

An interjection rarely consists of more than one word. Some of these words simply represent the sound you make:

> *Ah!, Ahem!, Eh?, er, Ha!, Hey!, Hm, Ho!, Ho-ho!, Mmm!, Oh!, Oi!, Ooh!, Oops!, Ouch!, Ow!, Phew!, Pooh!, Psst!, Shhh!, Tut-tut!, Ugh!, Uh-huh!, um, Whew!, Whoops!, Yippee!, Yuk!*

(*Ahem!* is supposed to represent the sound you make when you clear your throat, and *Tut-tut!* is supposed to represent the disapproving sound you make by clicking your tongue.)

Others are words that are also used as nouns, verbs, adjectives, etc.: *Cheers!, Great!, Help!, Thanks!*

In some cases, a word that began as an interjection has become adopted as a noun, verb, etc:

> *Boo!* → *The president was greeted with a chorus of **boos**.*
>
> *Hush!* → *There was a deathly **hush**.*
>
> *Pooh!* → *They **pooh-poohed** our idea.*
>
> *Shoo!* → *I **shooed** the geese away.*

Using interjections

Interjections are mainly used in spoken English. In written English they are rarely used except in direct speech.

Most interjections usually stand alone as minor sentences:

> *It'll do 180 miles an hour.–**Wow!***   *They eat worms and beetles.–**Ugh!***

However, they are often loosely attached to another sentence:

> ***Oops!** I've dropped the key!*   ***Shhh!** I'm trying to concentrate.*
>
> ***Oi!** Where do you think you're going?*   ***Mmm**, that smells nice!*

Some interjections may occur in the middle of a sentence, especially those that show hesitation:

*I think you've – **er** – forgotten something.*

*I've invited four people: John, Sue, Robin, and – **um** – Chris.*

Other types of interjection

There are a wide range of formulaic expressions that behave like interjections. These include:

- expressions of approval:

  Super!, Great!, Fab!, Cool!

- expressions of greeting, etc.:

  Hello!, Hi!, Goodbye!, Cheerio!

- drinking toasts:

  Cheers!, Bottoms up!, Skol!

- expressions of agreement or disagreement:

  Yes!, OK!, No!, No way!

- blasphemous or obscene expletives:

  Jesus!, God!, Hell!, Damn!, Shit!

- expressions of congratulation:

  Congratulations!, Well done!

- expressions of gratitude:

  Thank you!, Thanks!, Ta!, Cheers!

- expressions of contempt, disbelief, etc.:

  Rubbish!, Nonsense!, Bollocks!

WOTCHER, COCK!

The greeting *Wotcher!*, of Cockney origin, comes from the phrase *What cheer?*, formerly used in greeting friends or acquaintances. Other interjections that have evolved in a similar way include

Goodbye! (from *God be with you!*)
Howdy! (from *How do you do?*)
Strewth! (from *God's truth!*)

Cor blimey! (from *God blind me!*)
and the archaic *Zounds!* (from *God's wounds!*)

There are also a number of interjections used euphemistically in place of swear words, such as

Gee! (for *Jesus!*)
Crikey! (for *Christ!*)
Gosh! (for *God!*)

Sugar! (for *Shit!*)
and *Cobblers!* (for *Balls!*, from Cockney rhyming slang *cobbler's awls*)

Vocatives

A **vocative** is a word or phrase that makes it clear who you are talking to. It may be:

- the name of the person (or animal) you are talking to

  Mr Smith, *your visitors are here.*   *Get down,* **Rover!**

- a term that indicates a family relationship

  Mum, *have you seen my football boots anywhere?*
  Thanks, **Grandma**, *this is just what I need!*

- a term that indicates the occupation of the person you are talking to

  I get a pain in my back, **doctor**, *when I lie down.*
  Waiter, *there's a fly in my soup!*

- a word or phrase that shows respect, such as *sir, Your Highness*, etc.

  They will be ready on Saturday, **sir**.

- a word or phrase that shows disrespect, scorn, anger, etc.

  Get out of the way, **idiot!**   *Stop looking at my cards,* **cheat!**

- a term of endearment, such as *dear, darling, pet, my little one*, etc.

  Be careful, **darling!**

- a general term that includes a number of people

  Are you ready, **girls?**   *Come on,* **team**, *don't give up!*

- a phrase or clause containing *you*

  You with the red T-shirt, *what's your name?*
  Go away, **whoever you are!**

The use of vocatives

Vocatives are used for a number of purposes. They may

- attract the attention of the person you are talking to. In such cases the vocative is usually placed at the beginning of the sentence:

  Mr Smith, *your visitors are here.*   **Waiter**, *there's a fly in my soup!*

- indicate that you are talking to a particular person among a group. In such cases the vocative may be placed at the beginning, in the middle, or at the end of the sentence:

  Sue, I'd like you to sit here.   *Would you like a cup of tea, Dad?*

- be added simply to show affection, respect, annoyance, etc. In such cases the vocative is usually placed in the middle or at the end of the sentence:

  Come with me, dear, and I'll show   *They will be ready on Saturday, sir.*
  you where it is.   *Stop looking at my cards, cheat!*

Note that a vocative always has a comma before and/or after it in written or printed English. You can remove or add a vocative without affecting the grammatical structure of the sentence (though the meaning may be less clear).

OUT, DAMNED SPOT!

Inanimate nouns are sometimes used as vocatives, especially in literature. There are examples in the plays of Shakespeare:

Now boast thee, **death**, in thy possession lies / A lass unparallel'd. (*Antony and Cleopatra*, Act V Scene 2)

Frailty, thy name is woman! (*Hamlet*, Act I Scene 21)

Blow, **winds**, and crack your cheeks! (*King Lear*, Act III Scene 2)

Out, **damned spot**! (*Macbeth*, Act V Scene 1)

in the Bible:

Lift up your heads, **O ye gates**; and be ye lift up, **ye everlasting doors**. (*Psalm* 24:7)

O death, where is thy sting? **O grave**, where is thy victory? (*1 Corinthians* 15:55)

in the works of poets such as Chaucer, Keats, and Betjeman:

Go, **litel bok**, go, **litel myn tragedye**. (Geoffrey Chaucer, *Troilus and Criseyde*)

Thou, **silent form**, dost tease us out of thought /As doth eternity. (John Keats, *Ode on a Grecian Urn*)

Come, **friendly bombs**, and fall on Slough / It isn't fit for humans now. (Sir John Betjeman, *Slough*)

And in everyday life you may occasionally find yourself addressing an inanimate object with a vocative:

What's the matter, **you stupid machine**, why won't you work?

Come on, **sun**, stop hiding behind that cloud!

Nouns

What is a noun?

A **noun** is a word for a thing, feeling, state, person, animal, place, day, month, etc.:

car, circle, happiness, pain, freedom, rejection, nurse, Jack, dog, peacock, Quebec, Europe, Wednesday, July

Most nouns have different forms for singular and plural use:

car/cars, knife/knives, fungus/fungi

In a clause or sentence, most nouns have a word like *a, the, my, this,* etc., in front of them:

the car, your happiness, that dog

Types of noun

The six main types of noun are actually three pairs of opposites: proper nouns and common nouns, countable nouns and uncountable nouns, concrete nouns and abstract nouns.

• **proper nouns** name a specific person, place, etc., and have a capital letter at the beginning:

Jack, Quebec, January, Buddhism

• all other nouns are **common nouns**:

book, child, mud, granite, idea, surprise, impatience, knowledge

• **countable nouns** are nouns that can be made plural:

book/books, chair/chairs, idea/ideas, surprise/surprises

• **uncountable nouns** cannot be made plural:

mud but not **muds*   *impatience* but not **impatiences*
granite but not **granites*   *knowledge* but not **knowledges*

• **concrete nouns** refer to things you can see, touch, etc.:

book, child, mud, granite

• **abstract nouns** refer to feelings, qualities, states, etc., which you cannot see or touch:

idea, surprise, impatience, knowledge

Note that most nouns belong to more than one of the above groups: *book* is common, countable, and concrete; *knowledge* is common, uncountable, and abstract.

You will see from the following pages that some nouns can also be both countable and uncountable, or both concrete and abstract, depending on the sense in which you use them:

*The house backs onto a **wood**.*
  (countable)
*Did you follow the **instructions**?*
  (countable)
the **key** to the door (concrete)
a silver **chain** (concrete)

*The cabinet is made of **wood**.*
  (uncountable)
*a driver under **instruction***
  (uncountable)
the **key** to the mystery (abstract)
a **chain** of events (abstract)

WHERE IN THE WORLD DID THAT COME FROM?

Over the years, nouns have entered the English language from all parts of the world. Some are now firmly established, others are still regarded as newcomers. Here are some examples . . .

. . . from French: *abattoir, baton, casserole, debris, echelon, flair, gourmet, hotel, impasse, liaison, massage, negligee, parole, questionnaire, rapport, sabotage, toupee, valet.*

. . . from Italian: *aria, bravura, casino, diva, falsetto, graffiti, inferno, lasagne, minestrone, novella, oratorio, pizza, risotto, scenario, tempo, vendetta.*

. . . from German: *angst, blitz, delicatessen, frankfurter, glockenspiel, hinterland, kindergarten, leitmotiv, poltergeist, schnitzel, wanderlust.*

. . . from Spanish: *aficionado, bonanza, corral, embargo, fiesta, guerrilla, junta, machete, patio, rodeo, siesta, toreador, vigilante.*

. . . from Russian: *agitprop, balalaika, glasnost, intelligentsia, perestroika, sputnik, vodka.*

. . . from Japanese: *futon, geisha, hara-kiri, judo, karaoke, origami.*

. . . from Arabic: *fatwa, hookah, intifada, kebab, mufti, sheikh.*

. . . from Sanskrit: *ashram, karma, mantra, nirvana, yoga.*

. . . from Hindi: *chapati, dekko, guru, sari.*

. . . from Turkish: *caftan, dervish, kismet, yoghurt.*

. . . from Persian: *ayatollah, bazaar, khaki.*

Proper nouns and common nouns

Proper nouns are nouns that you use to name or refer to a specific person, place, institution, etc. They have a capital letter at the beginning:

Jane, Edward, Churchill, Mozart, Paris, January, Buddhism, Newsweek

All other nouns are common nouns:

boat, writer, hospital, thought, idealism, time

Proper nouns are different from common nouns in two ways:

- proper nouns do not usually have a plural, whereas most common nouns do: *books, cats*, but not **Londons, *Sandras*
- proper nouns are not generally used with *a/an* or *the* (unless it is part of the name), whereas common nouns are: *a book, an elephant, the cat*, but not **a London, *the Sandra*

In certain circumstances, however, proper nouns may behave like common nouns. In other words, they may be used with *a, an, the*, etc., or made plural:

*There are hundreds of **Smiths** in the phone book.* (= people called Smith)
*It's a **Degas**.* (= a painting by Degas)
*They played **the Mozart** at the end.* (= the piece by Mozart)
*You gave me this tie five **Christmases** ago.* (= at Christmas five years ago)
*There is **a Ms Lee** to see you.*
*I realized that it was no longer **the London** I had grown up in.*
*Which **Rochester** do you mean – the one in England or the one in America?*
*How many **Mondays** are there in May?*
*It was one of the coldest **Octobers** on record.*

Proper names

Proper nouns are sometimes called **proper names**, especially when they consist of more than one word. Sometimes both of these words are proper nouns in their own right, as in *Jane Austen, John Smith*. Sometimes one of the words is a common noun, adjective, etc., that is given a capital letter because it is part of the name, as in *Prince Charles, Oxford Street, New York, Southampton University*.

She married a **prince**. / *She married* **Prince Charles**.
I drove down the **street**. / *I drove down Oxford* **Street**.

Types of proper noun

Proper nouns (and proper names) include:

- names: *Sandra, Jim, Shakespeare*
- titles: *President Lincoln, Mrs Evans*
- forms of address: *Mum, Uncle Hugh*
- continents and countries: *Asia, Zimbabwe, Brazil, the Netherlands*
- states, counties, cities, towns, and villages: *California, Hampshire, Sydney, The Hague, Banbury, Ardentinny*
- mountains and mountain ranges: *Mount Everest, the Matterhorn, the Rocky Mountains, the Andes*
- islands and groups of islands: *Jamaica, the Isle of Man, the Bahamas*
- oceans, seas, lakes, rivers, and canals: *the Pacific (Ocean), the Mediterranean (Sea), Lake Geneva, Lake Michigan, the (River) Amazon, the (River) Thames, the Suez Canal, the Grand Union Canal*
- street names: *Oxford Street, London Road, Madison Avenue, the Strand*
- public buildings: *the White House, Buckingham Palace, Stoke Mandeville Hospital*
- months, days of the week: *January, Friday*
- languages: *English, French, Japanese, Urdu, Swahili*
- institutions, organizations, and facilities: *the British Broadcasting Corporation, the Central Intelligence Agency, the United Nations, Manchester Grammar School, the Savoy (Hotel), the Tate (Gallery)*
- events: *the Olympic Games, the French Revolution*
- festivals: *Christmas, Mardi Gras*
- religions: *Buddhism, Christianity*
- political parties: *the Labour Party, the Republican Party*
- newspapers, periodicals, and press agencies: *The Times, Newsweek, Reuters*

You may have noticed that in some of these categories – especially mountains, oceans, seas, rivers, and canals – many of the proper nouns are preceded by *the*. This does not usually have a capital letter unless it is a fixed part of the name, as in *The Hague*.

Countable nouns and uncountable nouns

A **countable noun** can be used with *a* or *an* in the singular, and can be counted or made plural:

a chair, chairs; an idea, ideas

An **uncountable noun** is not generally used with *a* or *an* in the singular, and cannot be counted or made plural:

mud but not **a mud* or **muds*
impatience but not **an impatience* or **impatiences*

(Note that some uncountable nouns are occasionally used with *a* or *an*, often with an adjective in between: *a knowledge of first aid; a formal education.*)

Both countable nouns and uncountable nouns can be used with *the, this, some*, and similar words:

The chair *collapsed as he sat down.* (countable)
*She wiped **the mud** off her boots.* (uncountable)
*What do you think of **this plan?*** (countable)
This information *could be very useful.* (uncountable)

Countable nouns are sometimes called **count nouns**. Uncountable nouns are sometimes called **uncount nouns, non-count nouns**, or **mass nouns**.

Other differences

Countable nouns must be used with a 'determiner' (e.g. *a, the, my, this,* etc.) in the singular, whereas uncountable nouns can stand alone:

A car *stopped outside.* not *****Car*** *stopped outside.* (countable)
*I've lost **my key**.* not **I've lost **key**.* (countable)
Advice *is too often ignored.* or ***Our advice*** *is too often ignored.*
    (uncountable)
*They asked for **help**.* or *They asked for **some help**.* (uncountable)

However, you can use singular countable nouns without a determiner in expressions like *in prison, at school, go to bed, go to church,* etc. In such expressions the countable noun behaves like an uncountable noun and cannot be made plural:

*while they were in **prison*** not **while they were in **prisons***
*people who go to **church** every Sunday* not **people who go to*
    churches *every Sunday*

Nouns that can be countable or uncountable

Many nouns have both countable and uncountable meanings or uses:

*We lit a **fire**.* (countable)	*He is afraid of **fire**.* (uncountable)
*The house backs onto a **wood**.* (countable)	*The cabinet is made of **wood**.* (uncountable)
*Did you follow the **instructions**?* (countable)	*a driver under **instruction*** (uncountable)
*Newborn **lambs** gambolled in the fields.* (countable)	*a joint of **lamb*** (uncountable)
*Two **coffees**, please.* (countable)	*a packet of **coffee*** (uncountable)
__emotions__ such as love, hate, joy, and sorrow (countable)	*Her voice was full of **emotion**.* (uncountable)
*He speaks several different **languages**.* (countable)	*__Language__ is a means of communication.* (uncountable)
*a **death** in the family* (countable)	*Heart disease is a common cause of **death**.* (uncountable)

In some of these examples the countable and uncountable meanings are closely related: *a death* (countable) is an instance of *death* (uncountable), and *a language* (countable) is a form of *language* (uncountable). In others the meanings are more distinct: *a wood* (countable) is a group of trees, whereas *wood* (uncountable) is a substance that comes from trees.

Nouns that are usually uncountable often have a countable sense meaning 'a type of . . .':

*He never drinks **wine** or spirits.* (uncountable)
*a book about the **wines** of Italy* (countable)
*a **wine** that goes well with fish* (countable)

*Please keep off the **grass**.* (uncountable)
*A **grass** that grows in sand dunes.* (countable)
*Edible **grasses** include wheat and other cereals.* (countable)

For other uncountable nouns, countable expressions can be formed with phrases meaning 'a piece of' or 'a quantity of':

a piece of advice	*a bit of luck*
a scrap of paper	*a grain of sand*
a shred of evidence	*a length of fabric*
a kilo of cheese	*a packet of flour*

Concrete nouns and abstract nouns

Concrete nouns refer to people, animals, or things that you can see, touch, etc.:

> child, elephant, grass, water, house, wood

Abstract nouns refer to actions, feelings, qualities, states, etc., which you cannot see or touch:

> idea, hate, pain, hope, knowledge, impatience, time

Many nouns have both concrete and abstract meanings or uses:

the **key** to the door (concrete)	the **key** to the mystery (abstract)
He played the whole piece without looking at the **music**. (concrete)	**Music** is the greatest of the arts. (abstract)
a silver **chain** (concrete)	a **chain** of events (abstract)
We found a box of old jazz **records** in the attic. (concrete)	She has broken several swimming **records**. (abstract)
Your **hands** are dirty. (concrete)	I gave him a **hand** with the washing up. (abstract)
She fell down the **steps**. (concrete)	The next **step** is to knead the dough. (abstract)
My **study** is at the back of the house. (concrete)	Entomology is the **study** of insects. (abstract)
The **heart** pumps blood round the body. (concrete)	the **heart** of the matter (abstract)

The abstract meaning is often just a figurative use of the concrete sense:

a **wave** of protest	a **shower** of praise
a **window** of opportunity	a **ceiling** on pay rises
the **road** to recovery	the **path** to success
a **wall** of suspicion	a **blanket** of gloom
the **machinery** of government	the **wheels** of change
a **mine** of information	a **fountain** of knowledge

Concrete and abstract common nouns

Both countable and uncountable common nouns may be either concrete or abstract.

Among concrete nouns, individual items (e.g. *hat, ship, bird, flower*) are usually countable nouns, whereas substances (e.g. *oxygen, flour, blood, granite*) are usually uncountable nouns.

Many abstract nouns – especially those ending in *-ness*, *-ment*, *-nce*, *-ion*, *-ity*, etc. – are uncountable nouns, but there are also many abstract countable nouns (e.g. *idea, mistake, attempt, dream*).

Concrete and abstract proper nouns

Like common nouns, proper nouns may be either concrete or abstract. Names of people, places, buildings, etc. (e.g. *Shakespeare, Brazil, the White House*) are concrete nouns. Names of months, days, languages, religions, etc. (e.g. *October, Monday, Urdu, Christianity*) are abstract nouns.

The formation of abstract nouns

Many abstract nouns are formed by adding a fixed ending to another word. These endings may be added

- to verbs:

shrink	+	*-age*	=	*shrinkage*	*mock*	+	*-ery*	=	*mockery*
betray	+	*-al*	=	*betrayal*	*sing*	+	*-ing*	=	*singing*
accept	+	*-ance*	=	*acceptance*	*connect*	+	*-ion*	=	*connection*
tempt	+	*-ation*	=	*temptation*	*manage*	+	*-ment*	=	*management*
exist	+	*-ence*	=	*existence*	*fail*	+	*-ure*	=	*failure*

- to adjectives:

real	+	*-ism*	=	*realism*	*bright*	+	*-ness*	=	*brightness*
solid	+	*-ity*	=	*solidity*	*warm*	+	*-th*	=	*warmth*

- to other nouns:

captain	+	*-cy*	=	*captaincy*	*infant*	+	*-icide*	=	*infanticide*
martyr	+	*-dom*	=	*martyrdom*	*hero*	+	*-ism*	=	*heroism*
child	+	*-hood*	=	*childhood*	*leader*	+	*-ship*	=	*leadership*

You will find more information about these fixed endings in the section 'Suffixes forming nouns' on page 68.

Singular and plural

A **singular** noun refers to one person, thing, etc.: *doctor, hat, suggestion*. A **plural** noun refers to more than one person, thing, etc.: *three doctors, several hats, many suggestions*.

Regular plurals

You can change most nouns from singular to plural by adding -*s*:

> *boat/boats, park/parks, game/games, path/paths, graph/graphs, toy/toys, donkey/donkeys, banana/bananas, taxi/taxis*

If the noun ends in -*ch*, -*sh*, -*ss*, -*zz*, or -*x*, you add -*es*:

> *church/churches, sash/sashes, dress/dresses, buzz/buzzes, fox/foxes*

If the noun ends in -*y*, and there is at least one consonant before the -*y*, you change the -*y* to -*ies*:

> *lady/ladies, city/cities, nappy/nappies, foundry/foundries*

All these plural forms are regular. In other words, they follow one of the three usual patterns in English: adding -*s*, adding -*es*, or changing -*y* to -*ies*.

Irregular plurals

There are also many nouns with irregular plural forms:

- -*oo*- changes to -*ee*- in *foot/feet, goose/geese, tooth/teeth*
- -*ou*- changes to -*i*- in *louse/lice, mouse/mice*
- -*an* changes to -*en* in *man/men, woman/women*
- -*en* is added in *child/children, ox/oxen*
- -*zes* is added in *fez/fezzes, quiz/quizzes*

Nouns ending in -f or -fe

Some nouns ending in -*f* or -*fe* change this ending to -*ves* in the plural:

> *calf/calves, half/halves, knife/knives, leaf/leaves, life/lives, loaf/loaves, shelf/shelves, thief/thieves, wife/wives, wolf/wolves*

Some just add -*s*, like a regular plural:

> *belief/beliefs, carafe/carafes, chief/chiefs, fife/fifes, gulf/gulfs, motif/motifs, oaf/oafs, proof/proofs, roof/roofs, safe/safes, waif/waifs*

Some can have *-fs* or *-ves*:

bulk: dwarf → dwarfs or dwarves

handkerchief → handkerchiefs or
    handkerchieves

hoof → hoofs or hooves

scarf → scarfs or scarves

wharf → wharfs or wharves

Nouns ending in -o

Some nouns ending in *-o* add *-es* in the plural:

echo/echoes, embargo/embargoes, hero/heroes, mosquito/mosquitoes,
motto/mottoes, potato/potatoes, tomato/tomatoes, volcano/volcanoes

Some just add *-s*, like a regular plural:

avocado/avocados, cameo/cameos, embryo/embryos, ghetto/ghettos,
piano/pianos, radio/radios, studio/studios

(Note that *-o* nouns that are short forms of longer nouns add *-s*, not *-es*,
in the plural: **demo**(*nstration*)/**demos**, **disco**(*theque*)/**discos**, **photo**(*graph*)/
photos, **hippo**(*potamus*)/**hippos**, **memo**(*randum*)/**memos**.)

Some can add *-s* or *-es*:

banjo → banjos or banjoes

cargo → cargos or cargoes

fresco → frescos or frescoes

grotto → grottos or grottoes

mango → mangos or mangoes

zero → zeros or zeroes

Nouns ending in -eau

Most English nouns ending in *-eau* are of French origin, and the plural
may be formed by adding *-s* or *-x*:

bureau → bureaus or bureaux

chateau → chateaus or chateaux

gateau → gateaus or gateaux

tableau → tableaus or tableaux

WOMEN AND CHILDREN FIRST!

The plurals of *woman* and *child* are not only irregular in form – the
sound of the word also changes.

    The *-o-* of *woman* sounds like the *-oo-* of *cook* or the *-u-* of *put*, but
the *-o-* of *women* sounds like the *-i-* of *kick* or *pit*. And the *-men* ending
of *women* rhymes with *win*, unlike the endings of *salesmen*, *snowmen*,
etc. The *-i-* of *child*, which rhymes with *filed*, changes to the 'short' *-i-*
of *chilled* in the plural form *children*.

{CONTD}

Plurals of nouns from Latin or Greek

Nouns ending in -a

Some nouns ending in -a change this ending to -ae in the plural: *alga/algae, larva/larvae, vertebra/vertebrae.*

Some just add -s, like a regular plural: *arena/arenas, era/eras, hernia/hernias, idea/ideas, quota/quotas, visa/visas.*

Some can have -as or -ae:

formula → *formulas* or *formulae*   *lacuna* → *lacunas* or *lacunae*

Nouns ending in -ex or -ix

Most nouns ending in -ex or -ix have a 'regular' plural that ends in -exes or -ixes: *complex/complexes, mix/mixes, prefix/prefixes, sex/sexes.*

But many also have an 'irregular' plural form in which -ex or -ix changes to -ices:

apex → *apexes* or *apices*   *index* → *indexes* or *indices*
appendix → *appendixes* or   *matrix* → *matrixes* or *matrices*
    appendices   *vertex* → *vertexes* or *vertices*

Nouns ending in -is

Many nouns ending in -is change this ending to -es in the plural: *axis/axes, basis/bases, crisis/crises, diagnosis/diagnoses, oasis/oases.*

But some have a 'regular' plural that ends in -ises: *dais/daises, ibis/ibises, iris/irises, metropolis/metropolises, trellis/trellises.*

Nouns ending in -on

Some nouns ending in -on change this ending to -a in the plural: *criterion/criteria, phenomenon/phenomena, spermatozoon/spermatozoa.*

Some just add -s, like a regular plural: *baton/batons, coupon/coupons, electron/electrons, polygon/polygons.*

Some can have -ons or -a:

automaton → *automatons* or *automata*

Nouns ending in -um

Some nouns ending in -um change this ending to -a in the plural: *bacterium/bacteria, datum/data, ovum/ova, spectrum/spectra, stratum/strata.*

Some just add *-s*, like a regular plural: *album/albums, conundrum/conundrums, museum/museums, pendulum/pendulums*.

Many can have *-ums* or *-a*:

aquariums → aquariums or aquaria
gymnasiums → gymnasiums or
    gymnasia

referendum → referendums or
    referenda
stadium → stadiums or stadia

Nouns ending in *-us*

Some nouns ending in *-us* change this ending to *-i* in the plural: *bacillus/bacilli, cumulus/cumuli, nucleus/nuclei, stimulus/stimuli*.

Some have a 'regular' plural that ends in *-uses*: *bonus/bonuses, chorus/choruses, foetus/foetuses, genius/geniuses, ignoramus/ignoramuses, sinus/sinuses, walrus/walruses*.

Some can have *-uses* or *-i*:

cactus → cactuses or cacti
focus → focuses or foci

radius → radiuses or radii
syllabus → syllabuses or syllabi

Which plural form should you use?

Where two plural forms are possible, the 'regular' one is often more common in everyday language and the 'irregular' one in scientific or technical usage:

a list of mathematical **formulae**
one of several peace **formulas** discussed at the conference

Sometimes the two plurals are totally interchangeable:

a shop selling **cactuses/cacti** and other house plants

Sometimes different plural forms are used in different senses:

The **media** [= newspapers, television, etc.] sometimes distort the facts.
Some people try to communicate with the dead through **mediums**.
The surgeon had removed six **appendixes** that week.
There are three useful **appendices** at the end of the book.

You may also find that dictionaries and other reference books do not always agree with each other on plural forms. Usage is constantly changing.

{CONTD}

Variable nouns

Most nouns are **variable** nouns – they have different forms in the singular and plural. Nouns that have only one form may be zero plurals or invariable nouns.

Zero plurals

A **zero plural** is a noun that has the same form in the singular and plural, such as *aircraft, barracks, crossroads, deer, headquarters, means, offspring, salmon, series, sheep*:

> **This aircraft** was designed by the same company.
> **These aircraft** were designed by the same company.
> She starred in **a** popular television **series**.
> She starred in **several** popular television **series**.

Many nationalities, such as *Chinese, Japanese, Portuguese, Swiss*, etc., are also zero plurals.

Some nouns with zero plural forms, especially names of animals, birds, and fish, may also have regular plural forms:

> a herd of **antelope(s)**   the **fish(es)** of the Atlantic Ocean

Many of these nouns also have an uncountable meaning, which is always singular:

> Fresh **fish** is sold here.   I've never eaten **pheasant**.

Invariable nouns

An **invariable** noun is either always singular or always plural, but not both. Singular invariable nouns include *mud* and *impatience*, and plural invariable nouns include *scissors* and *trousers*. You cannot have **muds, *impatiences, *a scissor*, or **a trouser*.

Singular invariable nouns

Some singular invariable nouns misleadingly end in *-s*, such as *aerobics, billiards, draughts* (the game), *linguistics, measles, mumps, news, physics, shingles* (the disease). They look like plural nouns, but they are not:

> **Aerobics is** a form of exercise. (not **Aerobics are* a form of exercise.)
> The **news was** not good. (not **The news were* not good.)

However, a number of nouns ending in *-ics* may be singular in some contexts and plural in others. These include *acoustics, economics, gymnastics, mathematics, politics, statistics, tactics*:

> **Acoustics is** the study of sound.
> The **acoustics** in the new hall **are** excellent.
> **Politics is** rarely discussed at these meetings.
> Her **politics were** revealed in the opening paragraph.

Some *-ics* words also have a singular form ending in *-ic*:

> This is **an** interesting **statistic**.
> **Statistics** is often studied in combination with mathematics.
> The accident **statistics have** not improved.
> I decided to try **a** different **tactic**.
> **Tactics is** the art of controlling military forces in battle.
> His **tactics were** somewhat unscrupulous.

Plural invariable nouns

Plural invariable nouns include *binoculars, cattle, dregs, folk, jeans, outskirts, people, remains, scissors, sunglasses, trousers, vermin*:

> The **cattle were** sold at auction. (not *The **cattle was** sold at auction.)
> The **people** concerned **have** been notified. (not The **people** concerned **has** been notified.)

Those ending in *-s* cannot be made singular by removing the *-s*:

> **dregs** of coffee (not *a **dreg** of coffee)
> I live in the **outskirts** of the village (not *I live in **an outskirt** of the village.)

However, some have a singular equivalent using 'a pair of':

> **These sunglasses are** the most expensive in the shop.
> **This pair of sunglasses is** the most expensive in the shop.

WRAPPED UP IN A FIVE-POUND NOTE

Words like *pound, metre, hundred, dozen*, etc., have a singular form with a plural meaning when they are used in front of a noun:

a five-**pound** note but It cost five **pounds**.
a six-**metre** length of timber but His garden is six **metres** longer than ours.
a three-**hour** wait but three **hours** later
four **hundred** books but **hundreds** of books
three **dozen** eggs but **dozens** of eggs

Similarly, *an eight-lane motorway, a four-course meal*, etc.

Collective nouns

A **collective noun** refers to a group of people, animals, etc., such as *committee, panel, jury, government, council, team, crew, family, audience, congregation, herd, flock, swarm, gang, horde, army*.

Singular or plural?

Collective nouns are singular in form, but you can use them with a singular verb or a plural verb:

> The **committee has** reached a decision at last.
> The **committee were** unable to agree on a new name for the club.

In the first example, the committee is a body of people acting together to make a joint decision. In the second example, it is a number of separate individuals who cannot agree with each other.

Here are some more pairs of examples:

> The **team has** never lost a home match.
> The **team were** disappointed at the result.
>
> The **audience was** not very large.
> The **audience were** given free tickets for another show.
>
> The **family has** caused a lot of trouble in the neighbourhood.
> The **family were** all present at the funeral.

Other words related to the collective noun may also be singular or plural:

> An **army** must always follow **its** leader.
> The **army** handed over **their** weapons.
>
> She wrote to the **council**, but **it** rejected her request for a grant.
> I would have phoned the **council**, but **they** don't work on Saturdays.

You may sometimes find it hard to decide whether to use a singular or plural verb, pronoun, etc., and it often doesn't matter which you choose. However, you should not mix singular and plural forms within the same sentence:

> The team **have** chosen Bob Jones as **their** captain. (not *The team **has** chosen Bob Jones as **their** captain. or *The team **have** chosen Bob Jones as **its** captain.)

Remember that the collective noun itself is singular, so it must be used with *this* or *that* rather than *these* or *those*, even if the verb is plural:

> **This** team are all university graduates. (not ***Those** team are all university graduates.)

However, most collective nouns can be made plural: *several committees, two teams*, etc. When you use a collective noun in the plural it behaves like any other plural noun:

> These families are most at risk.   Those herds will be destroyed.

Some collective nouns are uncountable. They cannot be made plural, but they may still be used with a singular or plural verb. Uncountable collective nouns include names of organizations, companies, etc.:

> **The BBC has** been accused of lowering its standards.
> **Ford are** working on a new model with improved fuel efficiency.

A BAZAAR OF GUILLEMOTS

There are a host of collective nouns for members of the animal kingdom. Here are some of the more common ones:

a colony of beavers	a pride of lions
a herd of cattle or deer	a school of porpoises or whales
a flock of sheep	a shoal of fish
a gaggle of geese	a swarm of bees
a pack of hounds or wolves	a troop of monkeys

There are also many that you will rarely (if ever) see or hear, except in lists of collective nouns. Here are some of the more picturesque ones:

a bazaar of guillemots	a murder of crows
a business of ferrets	a mutation of thrushes
a charm of goldfinches	a parliament of owls
a cloud of grasshoppers	a shrewdness of apes
a crash of rhinoceroses	a skulk of foxes
a deceit of lapwings	a singular of boars
a descent of woodpeckers	a sloth of bears
an exaltation of larks	a tittering of magpies
a mumble of moles	an unkindness of ravens

Gender of nouns

Most English nouns do not have a **gender**. In other words, they are neither masculine nor feminine.

(In many other languages all nouns have a gender. In French, for example, the word for 'garden' is masculine and the word for 'table' is feminine. The words used with them change accordingly: *un petit jardin* 'a little garden', *une petite table* 'a little table'. Other languages, such as Latin and German, also have a neuter gender.)

In English, the only words that change according to gender are the personal pronouns *he/him/himself* etc., *she/her/herself* etc., and *it/itself* etc. These usually reflect the natural gender or sex of the noun they refer to: *he* is used for male people and (some) male animals, *she* for female people and (some) female animals, and *it* for most other nouns:

> My **uncle** sold the car **he** won in the competition.
> **Valerie** wishes **she** had accepted the job.
> Whenever our **dog** hears a car go past, **he** barks.
> The **mouse** was not frightened; **it** didn't run away.
> The **house** is very old; **it** was built in the sixteenth century.

There are a number of exceptions to this basic rule:

- *it/itself* etc. is sometimes used for babies and young children, especially if the sex is not known or not relevant:

  > The **baby** next door is very quiet: **it** hardly ever cries.
  > When the **child** reaches this stage, **it** should be able to recognize letters and numbers.

- *she/her/herself* etc. is often used for boats and ships, sometimes for cars and other vehicles, and sometimes for countries:

  > The **boat** was badly damaged when **she** hit an underwater rock.
  > I bought my **car** a new battery, but **she** still wouldn't start.
  > **Spain** is less powerful now than **she** was then.

Animate nouns and inanimate nouns

Nouns referring to people and animals are called **animate** nouns:

> man, girl, doctor, teacher, cat, parrot, snake, frog, trout, wasp

All other nouns are **inanimate** nouns:

> *car, house, pen, cheese, water, love, happiness, possibility*

Animate nouns are further divided into **personal** nouns (for people) and **non-personal** nouns (for animals).

Dual gender

Some animate nouns have **dual gender**. This means that the same word is used for both sexes:

> *adult, child, parent, cousin, artist, singer, doctor, teacher, etc.*
> *cat, mouse, trout, spider, etc.*

Others have different forms for different sexes:

> *man/woman, boy/girl, husband/wife, prince/princess, hero/heroine,*
> *headmaster/headmistress, actor/actress, etc.*
> *bull/cow, dog/bitch, lion/lioness, cock/hen, drake/duck, etc.*

You will find more information about gender in the section 'Gender of pronouns' on page 126.

LADIES AND GENTLEMEN

In modern usage there is a trend away from 'gender-specific' nouns such as *headmaster/headmistress* and *author/authoress*. It is usually possible to find an alternative – you could replace *headmaster* and *headmistress* with *headteacher* (or *head*), and words like *author* can be used for either sex. Here are some more examples:

actor/actress → actor	*poet/poetess → poet*
manager/manageress → manager	*chairman/chairwoman → chairperson*
salesman/saleswoman → salesperson	or *chair*
spokesman/spokeswoman →	*policeman/policewoman → police*
spokesperson	*officer*

Similarly, you can often find alternatives for words or phrases containing the noun *man* in the sense of 'person' or 'people':

mankind → humankind	*spaceman → astronaut*
fireman → firefighter	*the man in the street → the average*
foreman → supervisor	*person*

Case of nouns

In Latin and some other languages, nouns have different forms for use as the subject, object, etc. This pattern of changes is called the **case** system. English does not have such a case system. The word *grass*, for example, has the same form as subject and object:

> **Grass** *is green.* (subject)   *Cows eat* **grass**. (object)

In both these sentences the word *grass* is in the **common case**.

The genitive case

When *'s* is added to an English noun to show possession, etc., the noun changes from the common case to the **genitive case**:

> *my* **son** (common case)   *my* **son's** *wife* (genitive case)

Most nouns add *'s* in the genitive case: *the child's toys, Jane's bike, the princess's uncle, Charles's friend.*

However, when the noun is plural and already ends in *-s*, the genitive ending is the apostrophe alone: *the students' tutor, the witches' broomsticks.* (Note that plural nouns that do not end in *-s*, such as *women, men,* and *children*, add *'s* in the genitive: *the children's toys.*)

For some singular nouns ending in *-s*, especially proper nouns, the genitive may be formed with *'s* or the apostrophe alone:

- single syllable names usually add *'s*:

> **James's** *dog*   *Mrs* **Jones's** *car*

- names of more than one syllable may add *'s* or *'*, depending on usage, the length of the word, the sound of the ending, etc.

> **Dickens's** *birthplace*   **Dumas's** *most famous works*
> **Hastings'** *tourist attractions*   **Archimedes'** *principle*

When a noun phrase is in the genitive case, the *'s* or *'* ending is attached to the last word, even if this is not the main noun of the phrase:

> *the head of state's entourage*   *somebody else's money*
> *the woman next door's television*   *the Prince of Wales's children*

The *of*-genitive and the double genitive

The genitive case usually shows possession. The noun in the genitive case is the person, animal, or thing that has or owns what follows:

Jack's house   **my dog's** tail
the car's wheels   **the town's** history

You can say the same thing using *of*, with the nouns in reverse order. This is called the *of*-genitive:

the house **of Jack**   the tail **of my dog**
the wheels **of the car**   the history **of the town**

The *of*-genitive is chiefly used for inanimate nouns and the genitive ending *'s* for animate nouns, especially for people: *the wheels of the car; Jack's house.*

Both *of* and the genitive ending *'s* or *'* are used in such phrases *as a friend of Michael's, some ideas of my colleagues'*, etc. This is called a **double genitive** or **post-genitive**.

Other uses of the genitive

The genitive ending does not always show possession. You can also use it

- in some fixed or descriptive phrases: *a **stone's** throw; at **arm's** length*
- in expressions of time: *four **hours'** work; in five **months'** time*
- to mean 'by' rather than 'of': ***France's** defeat of Spain* (= the defeat of Spain **by France**); ***the council's** rejection of the plan* (= the rejection of the plan **by the council**)

The local genitive and the independent genitive

There are two types of phrase in which the noun that follows a genitive may be left out. The first type is called the **local genitive**, because it usually refers to a place or location:

He went to **the doctor's**. (= the doctor's surgery)
The wedding was at **St Mary's**. (= St Mary's church)

The second type is called the **independent genitive**:

Peter's handwriting is neater than **Neil's**. (= Neil's handwriting)

You will find more information about case in the section 'Case of pronouns' on page 128.

Formation of nouns

New nouns may be formed in a number of ways. The three most common ways are:

- by adding a fixed ending, called a suffix, to another word:

  shrink + -age = shrinkage   *child + -hood = childhood*

- by adding a prefix at the beginning of another noun:

  dis- + appearance = disappearance   *un- + happiness = unhappiness*

- by joining two or more words together to make a compound noun:

  mouse + trap = mousetrap   *tooth + brush = toothbrush*

Suffixes forming nouns

A **suffix** is a fixed ending that you add to a word (or to part of a word) to form a new word.

- the suffixes *-age, -al, -ance, -ant, -ation, -ee, -ence, -er, -ery, -ing, -ion, -ment, -or, -ure,* etc., may be added to verbs:

  *block**age**, shrink**age**; betray**al**, refus**al**; accept**ance**, disappear**ance**; defend**ant**, depend**ant**; starv**ation**, tempt**ation**; employ**ee**, interview**ee**; exist**ence**, persist**ence**; driv**er**, us**er**; brew**ery**, mock**ery**; danc**ing**, writ**ing**; commun**ion**, translat**ion**; govern**ment**, manage**ment**; invest**or**, spectat**or**; depart**ure**, fail**ure***

- the suffixes *-cy, -ism, -ist, -ity, -ness,* etc., may be added to adjectives:

  *accura**cy**, vacan**cy**; real**ism**, spiritual**ism**; loyal**ist**, social**ist**; hostil**ity**, solid**ity**; bright**ness**, useful**ness***

- the suffixes *-age, -an, -cy, -dom, -eer, -ese, -ess, -ette, -ful, -hood, -ian, -icide, -ing, -ism, -ist, -ite, -let, -ling, -ship, -ster,* etc., may be added to other nouns:

  *line**age**, orphan**age**; Afric**an**, Europe**an**; captain**cy**, consultan**cy**; king**dom**, martyr**dom**; auction**eer**, profit**eer**; Japan**ese**, Malt**ese**; heir**ess**, manager**ess**; cigar**ette**, flannel**ette**; cup**ful**, sack**ful**; child**hood**, widow-**hood**; music**ian**, Paris**ian**; infant**icide**, pest**icide**; colour**ing**, floor**ing**; capital**ism**, hero**ism**; cartoon**ist**, violin**ist**; Israel**ite**, Trotsky**ite**; book**let**, drop**let**; duck**ling**, nest**ling**; leader**ship**, member**ship**; gang**ster**, song**ster***

Note that words ending in -*e* drop this letter before some suffixes:

refuse → *refusal*   *hostile* → *hostility*
translate → *translation*   *spectate* → *spectator*
dance → *dancing*

and words ending in -*t* or -*te* drop these letters before -*cy*:

accurate → *accuracy*   *consultant* → *consultancy*

Sometimes other letters are dropped, added, or changed:

Africa → *African*   *rely* → *reliance*
pronounce → *pronunciation*   *Malta* → *Maltese*
curious → *curiosity*   *responsible* → *responsibility*
evacuate → *evacuee*   *geology* → *geologist*

Prefixes

A **prefix** is a fixed group of letters that you add at the beginning of a word to form another word, usually with a different but related meaning.

The prefixes *de-*, *dis-*, *il-*, *im-*, *in-*, *ir-*, *non-*, *un-* give a noun the opposite meaning:

decentralization, **de**congestion, **dis**appearance, **dis**obedience, **il**legality, **il**literacy, **im**mortality, **im**probability, **in**ability, **in**convenience, **ir**regularity, **ir**relevance, **non**-existence, **non**-violence, **un**happiness, **un**tidiness

Other prefixes include:

anti- **anti**cyclone, **anti**histamine
counter- **counter**attack,
   countermeasure
ex- **ex**-husband, **ex**-president
fore- **fore**arm, **fore**shore
hyper- **hyper**inflation,
   hypersensitivity
inter- **inter**action, **inter**marriage
mega- **mega**byte, **mega**watt;
   megabucks, **mega**star

macro- **macro**economics,
   macrophotography
micro- **micro**film, **micro**wave
mis- **mis**management, **mis**spelling
over- **over**eating, **over**work
re- **re**-creation, **re**-delivery
semi- **semi**circle, **semi**final
super- **super**glue, **super**hero
vice- **vice**-chancellor,
   vice-president

You will find more information about prefixes and suffixes in the section 'Formation of adjectives' on page 104.

{CONTD}

Compound nouns

A **compound noun** is made up of two or more other words, at least one of which is usually a noun. These words may be joined together or linked by a hyphen. Some compound nouns are always written as one word, some never. For many others you will find that opinions vary – some dictionaries print them with a hyphen, some without.

Here are some of the most frequent types of compound noun:

- noun + noun: *air force, bookshop, coffee table, dinner jacket, eye-opener, footstool, goalkeeper, holidaymaker, inkwell, jet set, keyhole, life belt, mousetrap, newspaper, opera glasses, pocket money, question mark, rabble-rouser, seaweed, toothbrush, umbrella stand, vantage point, waistline, xylophone player, youth club, zebra crossing*

- noun + adjective: *court martial, knight errant, mother superior, poet laureate, secretary-general*

- adjective + noun: *black eye, double glazing, goodwill, half-truth, split second*

- noun + adverb: *hanger-on, passer-by*

- verb + adverb: *breakdown, flyover, knockout, shake-up, spin-off*

- noun + preposition or conjunction + noun: *gin and tonic, man-of-war, father-in-law, sergeant at arms*

- adverb or preposition + noun: *aftereffect, afterthought; downside, downturn; inlet, insight; offcut, offshoot; overcoat, overhang; underclothes, underpass*

- single letter + noun: *T-shirt, U-turn, x-ray*

- other combinations: *down-and-out, forget-me-not, has-been, also-ran*

A compound noun behaves like a single noun, no matter how many words it consists of. You can usually make its main noun plural (e.g. *two black eyes*), but its other parts are fixed – you cannot have a **blacker eye*.

The plural of compound nouns

The plural of compound nouns is usually formed by making the noun part plural:

*knight**s** errant, secretar**ies**-general; black eye**s**, half-truth**s**; hanger**s**-on, passer**s**-by; aftereffect**s**, overcoat**s**, T-shirt**s**, X-ray**s***

In 'noun + noun' compounds, only the second noun is made plural:

> dinner jacket**s** (not *dinner**s** jacket or *dinner**s** jacket**s**)
> footstool**s** (not ***feet**stool or ***feet**stool**s**)

In 'noun + preposition + noun' compounds, the first noun is made plural:

> **men**-of-war (not *man-of-war**s**)

In 'noun + conjunction + noun' compounds, the second noun is made plural:

> gin and tonic**s** (not *gin**s** and tonic)

In compounds that do not contain a noun, the final part is made plural:

> breakdown**s**, spin-off**s**; down-and-out**s**, forget-me-not**s**, has-been**s**

Note that there are some exceptions to these rules. For example, *court martial, mother superior,* and *father-in-law* have two possible plurals – *courts martial* or *court martials, mothers superior* or *mother superiors,* and *fathers-in-law* or *father-in-laws.*

'TWAS BRILLIG, AND THE SLITHY TOVES ...

This is a line from Lewis Carroll's *Through the Looking-Glass.* Carroll was fond of coining new words. Here he combined *lithe* and *slimy* to form *slithy* and later explained 'It's like a portmanteau – there are two meanings packed up into one word.'

Carroll's explanation has given us the term **portmanteau word** for a new word coined by blending together parts of other words. (A portmanteau word is also called a **blend**). The noun *motel,* for example, combines *motor* with *hotel* to form a word meaning 'a hotel for motorists'.

A similar development has led to nouns like *workaholic* and *chocoholic,* formed by blending *work* and *chocolate* with *alcoholic.* Sometimes the ending of one noun is added to others to form a whole range of new words. The *Watergate* scandal of 1972, for example, has given rise to terms like *Irangate, Camillagate,* etc. And the term *newspeak,* coined by George Orwell in his novel *1984,* has given rise to *computerspeak, winespeak,* etc.

The noun phrase

A **noun phrase** is a group of words that contains a noun or pronoun:

a house   *all those books*
the old black dog   *something new*

A noun phrase may be the subject, object, or complement of a clause or sentence:

Those shoes *are too expensive.* (subject)
They bought **four tickets**. (direct object)
She gave **the child** *a drink.* (indirect object)
He is **an English teacher**. (complement)

A noun phrase may also consist of a single word, such as *cats, mice,* or *they* in the following sentences:

Cats *chase* **mice**.   **They** *are cold.*

The head noun

The main noun of a noun phrase is called the **head noun**. Most noun phrases are made up of a head noun with another word or words before and/or after it.

The word or words used before the head noun may be:

- a word like *a, the, my, this, one, some,* etc. (called a determiner):

  a *house*   **some** *clothes*
  all those *books*   **my three** *sisters*

- an adjective (or a word used like an adjective):

  new *cars*   **worrying** *news*
  shiny brown *shoes*   **garden** *tools*

- a combination of these:

  the old black *dog*   **all our good** *intentions*

The word or words used after the head noun may be:

- a phrase beginning with a preposition:

  people **from London**   *the shop* **on the corner**
  the money **in your pocket**   *cats* **without tails**

- a type of clause:

  *the school **where I teach***   *boots **covered in mud***
  *those **who can't swim***   *children **wearing jeans***

- an adjective or adverb:

  *somebody **new***   *the sky **above***

Some noun phrases contain more than one noun: *the shop on the corner;* ***boots covered in mud***. In these two examples the head nouns are *shop* and *boots*. The head noun is the one that must stay if the sentence as a whole is to make sense:

  *My parents own the **shop** on the corner.*
  *My parents own the **shop**.* (not **My parents own the **corner**.*)

If the noun phrase is the subject of a clause or sentence, the head noun is the one that the verb agrees with:

  *The **books** on this shelf **are** his.* (not **The books on this **shelf** is his.*)
  *The **car** with flat tyres **is** hers.* (not **The car with flat **tyres** **are** hers.*)

When a pronoun is the head of a noun phrase, it usually stands alone – the pronoun *is* the noun phrase:

  ***She** hates **me**.*   ***That** looks nice!*

However, a noun phrase may consist of a head pronoun followed by other words:

  ***He who hesitates** is lost.*   ***Some of the cards** are missing.*

Simple noun phrases and complex noun phrases

There are two types of noun phrase: simple noun phrases and complex noun phrases. A **simple** noun phrase consists of a single noun or pronoun, or a noun preceded by a word like *a, the, my, this*, etc.:

  trees; them; an apple; the car; our friends; that book

All other noun phrases are **complex** noun phrases:

  these ancient oak trees   *the car outside*
  the shop on the corner   *his youngest daughter*

The phrase *the shop on the corner* is a complex noun phrase containing two simple noun phrases, *the shop* and *the corner*, linked by the preposition *on*.

Determiners and modifiers

What is a determiner?

A **determiner** is a word like *a, the, my, this, some,* or *many*. It tells you how much, how many, which, whose, etc. Determiners come at the beginning of a noun phrase. They may come directly before the noun, or there may be an adjective between the determiner and the noun.

There are several groups of determiners:

- the words *a, an,* and *the,* called articles.
- words showing possession, called possessives: *my, your, his, her, its, one's, our, their.*
- words showing which person or thing you are talking about, called demonstratives: *this, that, these, those.*
- words asking which person or thing you are talking about, called interrogatives: *what, which, whose.*
- cardinal numerals: *one, two, three, four, five, six,* etc.
- ordinal numerals: *first, second, third, fourth,* etc.
- fractions: *half, one-third, three-quarters,* etc.
- words that tell you how many times, called multipliers: *double, twice.*
- words that tell you how much or how many, called quantifiers: *all, every, each, both, some, any, no, several, enough, many, much, more, most, a few, few, fewer, fewest, a little, little, less, least, either, neither, a bit of, a lot of, lots of, plenty of, a great deal of, a good deal of,* etc.
- various other words: *such, what, other, another,* etc.

Using determiners with countable and uncountable nouns

A countable noun is a noun that can be made plural: *book* is a singular countable noun and *books* is a plural countable noun. An uncountable noun – such as *rice* – cannot be made plural.

You can use some determiners with all types of noun – singular countable nouns, plural countable nouns, and uncountable nouns:

the book, **the** books, **the** rice	**any** book, **any** books, **any** rice
my book, **my** books, **my** rice	**what** book, **what** books, **what** rice
no book, **no** books, **no** rice	

Other determiners can be used with singular countable nouns and uncountable nouns, but not with plural countable nouns:

this book, **this** rice	**that** book, **that** rice

Others can be used with plural countable nouns and uncountable nouns, but not with singular countable nouns:

all books, **all** rice	**most** books, **most** rice
some books, **some** rice	**a lot of** books, **a lot of** rice
enough books, **enough** rice	**plenty of** books, **plenty of**
more books, **more** rice	rice

(Note that *some* can be used with a singular countable noun to mean 'a remarkable', 'an unspecified', etc., as in *That's **some** bruise you've got on your leg!* or *I read about it in **some** magazine or other*.)

Finally, there are a number of determiners that you can only use with one type of noun:

- only with singular countable nouns: *a book, an idea, one book, every book, each book, either book, neither book.*

- only with plural countable nouns: *these books, those books, two books* (also other cardinal numerals), *both books, several books, many books, few books, fewer books, fewest books, a few books.*

- only with uncountable nouns: *much rice, little rice, less rice, least rice, a little rice, a bit of rice, a great deal of rice.*

Determiner or pronoun?

Many words can be used as determiners or pronouns:

*Take **this** key.* (determiner)	*Take **this**.* (pronoun)
*I've had **some** tea.* (determiner)	*I've had **some**.* (pronoun)
***All** the books were destroyed.* (determiner)	***All** were destroyed.* (pronoun)
*He gave **half** the money to his sister.* (determiner)	*He gave **half** to his sister.* (pronoun)

As a general rule: if the word has a noun after it, then it is a determiner. If this noun has been left out, then the word is a pronoun.

There is an exception to this rule: if the word is separated from the noun by *of*, then it is a pronoun, not a determiner.

*   ***Some** of my photos are missing.* (pronoun)
*   ***Many** of her answers were wrong.* (pronoun)
*   ***All** of the books were destroyed.* (pronoun)
*   *He gave **half** of the money to his sister.* (pronoun)
*   ***Both** of the men wore gloves.* (pronoun)

Types of determiner

There are three types of determiner:

- central determiners, as in *an hour, the music, her sons, our problems*
- predeterminers, which come before the central determiner: *half an hour, all the music*
- postdeterminers, which come after the central determiner: *her two sons, our many problems*

Central determiners

Central determiners include the articles, possessives, demonstratives, interrogatives, and some quantifiers (such as *every, each, some, any, no, enough, either, neither*): *a car, **the** rain, **her** house, **those** children, **which** book, **every** day, **some** cheese, **no** luck, **either** chair*

You cannot normally use two central determiners next to each other in the same noun phrase. The word *every* is an exception – it sometimes comes after a possessive, as in ***my every word*** or ***their every need***.

You will find more information about central determiners in the sections 'Articles' on page 80, 'Possessives' on page 118, 'Demonstratives' on page 120, and 'Interrogatives' on page 120.

Predeterminers

A **predeterminer** is a determiner that comes before the central determiner. Predeterminers include:

- fractions: *half, one-third, three-quarters*, etc.
- multipliers (words that tell you how many times): *double, twice*, etc.
- some quantifiers (words that tell you how much or how many): *all, both, such . . . !, what . . . !*

Here are some examples, with the predeterminers in bold type:

> **half** an hour   **both** my children
> **double** your salary   **what** a waste!

Note that you can use *all* and *both* either on their own before the noun or with *the, my*, etc.:

> **All** cats are mammals.   **Both** parents must sign the form.
> **All** the cats in my road are black.   **Both** her parents were present.

Postdeterminers

A **postdeterminer** is a determiner that comes after the central determiner in a noun phrase. Postdeterminers include

- cardinal numerals: *one, two, three, four, five, six,* etc.
- ordinal numerals: *first, second, third, fourth, fifth, sixth,* etc.
- the words *last* and *next*
- some quantifiers: *several, many, much, more, most, few, fewer, fewest, little, less, least*

Here are some examples, with the postdeterminers in bold type:

her **two** sons	no **more** money
the **fifth** time	these **few** words
his **next** visit	what **little** information

Some postdeterminers can be used together before the noun:

the **first six** applicants	**one last** attempt
our **next few** visits	**several more** opportunities

Note that you can also use most of these words on their own before the noun:

Three people are missing.	**Most** children like ice cream.
I have **several** friends in Paris.	She has **few** commitments.
Many cars are unroadworthy.	He has **less** money than you.

But the ordinal numerals (*first, second, third,* etc.) are rarely used on their own in this way.

You will find more information about cardinal and ordinal numerals on page 82.

FEWER OR LESS?

Using *less* or *least* instead of *fewer* or *fewest* is a common mistake. As a general rule, *less* and *least* should be used before singular nouns, while *fewer* and *fewest* are used before plural nouns:

less time and **fewer** opportunities
less traffic and **fewer** people
the least effort and the **fewest** achievements
the least land and the **fewest** cattle

Articles

The words *a*, *an*, and *the* are called **articles**. They come before a noun:

> **a** *shirt*; **an** *event*; **the** *writing*

There are often other words between the article and the noun:

> **a** *white shirt*   **a** *neatly ironed shirt*
> **an** *important event*   **an** *extremely rare event*
> **the** *untidy writing*   **the** *very small writing*

The indefinite article and the definite article

There are two types of article:

- the **indefinite article** (*a*/*an*): *a thought, an icicle.*
- the **definite article** (*the*): *the book, the animals.*

The indefinite article has two forms:

- *a* is used before a consonant sound: *a horse, a useful tool.*
- *an* is used before a vowel sound: *an open door, an heir, an X-ray, an MP.*

Note that it is the first *sound* of the word that matters. Some vowels have the sound of a consonant (such as the *u-* of useful, which sounds like the *y-* of you), so they are used with the indefinite article *a*. Some words begin with a silent consonant (such as *heir*, which is pronounced like the word *air*), so they are used with *an*.

You will sometimes see *an* before words beginning with an *h* that is not silent, as in *an hotel* or *an historic event*. This is rather old-fashioned, but it is no more or less correct than *a hotel* and *a historic occasion*.

Using the articles

You generally use *the* for a particular person or thing, whereas *a*/*an* is less specific:

> *Bring me **a** pen.* (= any pen)
> *Bring me **the** pen with a white cap.*
> *You'll find a pen and a pencil on my desk: bring me **the** pen.*

You generally use *a*/*an* for one of several people or things, and *the* when there is only one:

*I've found **a** way out.* / *I've found **the** way out.*
*We went to York last weekend: on Saturday we visited **a** craft centre and on Sunday we visited **the** cathedral.*

Sometimes you use *the* when you are thinking of a particular example, though there may be more than one: *I need to go to **the** bank.*

You can use *a/an* before singular nouns, but not before plural nouns. You can use *the* before both singular and plural nouns:

A leaf *fell from the tree.* / **Leaves** *fell from the tree.*
The train *is running late.* / **The trains** *are running late.*

You can also use *the* with a singular noun to refer to a whole group of people, animals, or things:

The ant *is a social insect.*   **The working parent** *needs these*
The pine tree *is grown for timber.*   *facilities.*

You can also use *a/an* to mean 'one' or 'per':

a *month ago*   *70 miles **an** hour*

The zero article

The **zero article** is where the article is left out altogether, e.g. before a plural or uncountable noun in a general statement:

Pine trees *are grown for **timber**.*   **Working parents** *need these*
Money *makes the world go round.*   *facilities.*

The zero article also occurs in some phrases containing countable nouns:

*travel by **bus**, go to **school**, stay for **dinner**, in **hospital**, at **home***

Articles are not generally used in front of proper nouns, but they may sometimes come before a name:

*I had a letter from **a** Jane Carter.* (= from somebody called Jane Carter, a name that means nothing to me)
*I had a letter from Michael Jackson – not **the** Michael Jackson, of course!* (= from Michael Jackson, who is somebody I know, but who is not the famous singer Michael Jackson)

When you use the word *the* like this, you pronounce it like the word *thee*. This emphatic pronunciation is also sometimes used with common nouns:

*If you want to learn about grammar, this is **the** book to read!*

Numerals

The term **numeral** is used in grammar for words like *one*, *two*, *three*, etc., and *fourth*, *fifth*, *sixth*, etc. This is to avoid confusion with the term **number**, which tells you whether a word is singular and plural.

There are two types of numeral:

- the **cardinal numerals**: *one, two, three, sixteen, seventeen, twenty-four, eighty-five, nine hundred, one million*, etc.

- the **ordinal numerals**: *first, second, third, eighteenth, nineteenth, thirty-sixth, seventy-fifth, four hundredth, thousandth*, etc.

Most ordinal numerals are formed by adding *-th* to the end of the cardinal numeral:

> four/**fourth**, thirteen/**thirteenth**, sixty-seven/**sixty-seventh**, two hundred/**two hundredth**

(Note that it is the very last word of the cardinal numeral that takes this ending: *eight hundred and fifty-six* → *eight hundred and fifty-sixth*.)

Some ordinals are totally irregular: *one/**first**, two/**second**, three/**third***.

Others change or drop the last letter(s) of the cardinal: *five/**fifth**, twelve/**twelfth**; eight/**eighth**, nine/**ninth**; twenty/**twentieth**, thirty/**thirtieth**,* etc.

(Note that when *one, two, five, eight, twelve*, etc., are at the end of a larger numeral, the ordinal remains irregular: *sixty-two* → *sixty-second*; *three hundred and twelve* → *three hundred and **twelfth**.*)

When cardinals and ordinals are used together, the ordinal usually comes before the cardinal:

> the **first two** novels on the list (i.e. the first novel on the list and the second novel on the list)

In special circumstances the cardinal may come first:

> the **two first** novels on the list (i.e. the two novels on the list that are the first novels written by their authors)

Numerals as determiners, pronouns, or nouns

Numerals are usually determiners or pronouns. If the numeral has a noun straight after it, then it is a determiner. If this noun has been left out, or if it separated from the numeral by *of*, then the numeral is a pronoun.

my **three** *children* (determiner)	**three** *of my children* (pronoun)
six hundred *bricks* (determiner)	*I gave her* **six hundred**. (pronoun)
the **fourth** *attempt* (determiner)	*the* **fourth** *of his many attempts* (pronoun)
their **twenty-fifth** *anniversary* (determiner)	*the* **twenty-fifth** *in the queue* (pronoun)

Cardinal numerals may also be nouns:

I drew a large **nine** *on the front.*   *There are no* **sixes** *in the number.*

When ordinal numerals are used as nouns, they usually refer to fractions:

a **third** *of the population*   *She divided the cake into* **fifths**.

Here are some other special uses of numerals:

- for decades: *at the end of the* **eighties**; *a woman in her* **forties**.
- in titles: *Henry the* **Fifth**.
- in dates: *the* **twenty-ninth** *of May*; *She left on the* **tenth**.

How we say numerals

How we say a cardinal numeral depends on what we are talking about. For example, the numeral 1800 may be called *one thousand eight hundred* or *eighteen hundred*. As the year 1800 it is usually *eighteen hundred*. As a telephone number it could be *one eight double oh* or *one eight double zero*. Even with dates we are not altogether consistent: we say *ten sixty-six* for 1066 but *two thousand and one* for 2001.

NOTHING DOING

The numeral *0* has many names: *zero, nought, nothing,* the slang terms *zilch* and *zip,* and the old-fashioned *cipher,* for example. In sports such as tennis and badminton it is called *love,* in cricket it is a *duck,* while in other sports it is usually *nil.* And when said as part of a longer number, it is often called *oh.*

–10° (ten degrees below **zero**)

a car that can accelerate from 0–60 (**nought** *to sixty) in under seven seconds*

0.4 (**nought** *point four) but .04 (point* **oh** *four)*

James Bond, 007 (double **oh** *seven)*

in 1906 (nineteen **oh** *six)*

serving for the match at 40–0 (forty **love**)

a score of 2–0 (two **nil**)

Modifiers

In a noun phrase, the words that come before or after the noun and tell you more about it are called **modifiers**. There are two types of modifier: premodifiers and postmodifiers.

Premodifiers

Premodifiers are modifiers that come before the noun. They are usually adjectives:

the **old** wardrobe
a **traditional French** recipe

my **favourite** aunt
shiny brown shoes

Other types of premodifier include:

- the -*ing* form or -*ed* form of a verb, used like an adjective. These are sometimes called participial adjectives, because they have the same form as the present or past participle of the verb.

a **fading** memory
faded jeans
worrying news
a **worried** expression

the **coming** months
his **broken** dreams
the **winning** team
her **swollen** wrist

- a noun or noun phrase used like an adjective. These are sometimes called adjectival nouns.

the **village** church
garden tools
a **jam** tart

an **art school** student
city-centre traffic congestion
a **Church of England** vicar

- a noun or noun phrase with the genitive ending 's or '

a **children's** book
a **dog's** life

Michael's car
an **old wives'** tale

- an adverb used like an adjective or before a pronoun

the **then** president
the **above** illustration
inside information
a **downstairs** room

virtually everything
absolutely nothing
hardly anyone
almost nobody

- a phrase beginning with a preposition

an **under-the-counter** payment
behind-the-scenes negotiations

- a clause

a ***keep-fit*** *class*	a ***never-to-be-forgotten*** *experience*
a ***do-it-yourself*** *shop*	a ***save-as-you-earn*** *scheme*
a ***come-hither*** *look*	*She gave me a* **'*wouldn't you***
a ***devil-may-care*** *attitude*	***like to know'*** *smile.*

Note that phrases and clauses are often hyphenated as premodifiers:

    a ***middle-class*** *family*   a ***well-paid*** *job*

This may avoid ambiguity: compare *the best-known cure* (i.e. the most famous cure) with *the best known cure* (i.e. the best cure that is known).

Using more than one premodifier

You can use several premodifiers together, sometimes with commas in between:

six **hot, tired, hungry** *children*	a ***rusty old iron*** *bar*
her **smart grey school** *uniform*	a ***very puzzled German*** *tourist*

Adjectives may have an adverb in front of them:

this **very dangerous** *task*	*several* **potentially embarrassing**
my **freshly ironed** *shirt*	*questions*

You will find more information about premodifiers in the section 'Adjectives' beginning on page 96.

POETIC LICENCE

Poets are very fond of stringing adjectives and other premodifiers together for effect:

Wee, sleekit, cow'rin, tim'rous beastie. (Robert Burns, 'To a Mouse')

. . . the sloeblack, slow, black, crowblack, fishingboat-bobbing sea. (Dylan Thomas, *Under Milk Wood*, J M Dent)

Villon, our sad bad glad mad brother's name. (Algernon Charles Swinburne, *Ballad of François Villon*)

An old, mad, blind, despised, and dying king. (Percy Bysshe Shelley, *Sonnet: England in 1819*)

A poor, infirm, weak, and despis'd old man. (William Shakespeare, *King Lear*, Act III Scene 2)

{CONTD}

Postmodifiers

Postmodifiers are modifiers that come after the noun. They include:

- adjectives

  *the heir **apparent***   *someone **new***
  *the village **proper***   *nobody **famous***

- adjective phrases

  *a woman **confident of success***   *the bank **closest to my office***
  *a man **older than me***   *homes **cheap enough for all***

- adverbs

  *the sky **above***   *the car **behind***
  *the man **outside***   *the way **in***

- prepositional phrases (i.e. phrases beginning with a preposition)

  *people **from London***   *the shop **on the corner***
  *a girl **with red hair***   *a present **for my friend***

- relative clauses (i.e. clauses beginning with *that, which,* etc.)

  *the people **who live here***   *the school **where I teach***
  *the clothes **that they wore***   *the car **in which he came***

- non-finite clauses (i.e. clauses containing the present participle (*-ing*
  form), past participle (*-ed* form), or infinitive of a verb)

  *a child **wearing a baseball cap***   *an essay **to write***
  *boots **covered in mud***   *money **to spend***

- appositive clauses (you will find more information about these on
  page 93)

  *the fact **that the reviewer had***   *the idea **that computers could***
  *   **not seen the film***   ***take the place of books***

Using more than one postmodifier

A noun phrase may contain more than one postmodifier:

  *the car I **behind** I **with a faulty headlight***
  *anything I **valuable** I **that isn't insured***
  *a girl I **with red hair** I **wearing a bikini***

In the three examples above, both postmodifiers tell you more about the head noun of the noun phrase:

> the car **behind** / the car **with a faulty headlight**
> anything **valuable** / anything **that isn't insured**
> a girl **with red hair** / a girl **wearing a bikini**

However, the second postmodifier does not always refer back to the head noun. Sometimes it tells you more about the noun at the end of the first postmodifier:

> a factory | employing fifty people | **from the local community**
> a factory employing **fifty people from the local community**
>
> an old tree | in the village | **where my uncle lives**
> an old tree in **the village where my uncle lives**

This may cause ambiguity. In the phrase *the car parked outside the house with a broken window,* is it the car or the *house* that has a broken window? Such ambiguity can sometimes be resolved by reordering the postmodifiers: *the car with a broken window parked outside the house.*

DANGLING MODIFIERS AND HANGING PARTICIPLES

A modifier should be placed as close as possible to the word or phrase it relates to. If you move a modifying phrase or clause to the beginning of the sentence, the effect may be unintentionally humorous:

Wearing nothing but his underpants, she watched him dive into the river.
Solidly built from local stone, the villagers will oppose any plans to demolish the old schoolhouse.

This is called a dangling, hanging, or misrelated modifier. (Or, if the offending clause contains a participle, it may be called a dangling, hanging or misrelated participle.)

Sometimes the effect is merely ambiguous: *Born in 1950, Anna's father was a musician.* Was it Anna or her father who born in 1950? If it was *Anna,* the sentence should be rephrased: *Born in 1950, Anna was the daughter of a musician.*

It is therefore best to avoid dangling modifiers and hanging participles, despite their occasional use in literature:

Sleeping in mine orchard, a serpent stung me. (William Shakespeare, *Hamlet*, Act I Scene 5)

Relative clauses

A **relative clause** is a clause beginning with *that, which, who, whom, whose, when, where*, etc. The words *that, which, who, whom,* and *whose* are called relative pronouns. The words *when* and *where* are relative adverbs.

A relative clause usually comes after a noun and tells you more about it:

the clothes **that they wear**

this ring, **which belonged to my grandmother**, ...

the people **who live here**

the school **where I teach**

the man **whom she married**

the woman **whose car had been stolen**

a day **when nothing went right**

The relative pronouns *which* and *whom* are sometimes preceded by a preposition:

the paper **in which** it was wrapped

an old building **about which** little is known

the person **to whom** the letter is addressed

the man **with whom** she arrived

You can often replace the relative adverbs *when* and *where* with *at which, in which, on which*, etc.:

a day **on which** nothing went right   the school **at which** I teach

Restrictive clauses and non-restrictive clauses

There are two types of relative clause: restrictive clauses and non-restrictive clauses.

A **restrictive** clause (also called a **defining** clause) gives essential information, and cannot be removed without making the meaning unclear.

A **non-restrictive** clause (also called a **non-defining** clause) gives information that is not essential and that can be left out.

Here are two examples:

I have two sons and two daughters; my daughter **who lives in Kent** is a doctor. (restrictive)

I have a son and a daughter; my daughter, **who lives in Kent**, is a doctor. (non-restrictive)

In the first sentence, the restrictive clause *who lives in Kent* tells you which of my two daughters is a doctor. If the clause is removed, this is no longer clear:

> *I have two sons and two daughters; my daughter is a doctor.* (Which daughter?)

In the second sentence the non-restrictive clause *who lives in Kent* is not needed, because I only have one daughter:

> *I have a son and a daughter; my daughter is a doctor.*

Here are some more pairs of examples:

> *The umbrella **that I left on the train** was a birthday present.* (restrictive)
> *The umbrella, **which I left on the train**, was a birthday present.* (non-restrictive)
>
> *The bullet **that killed him** came from this gun.* (restrictive)
> *The bullet – **which killed him** – came from this gun.* (non-restrictive)
>
> *This uncle **whom I have never met** is very rich.* (restrictive)
> *This uncle, **whom I have never met**, is very rich.* (non-restrictive)

Note that non-restrictive clauses are usually separated from the rest of the sentence by a pair of commas or dashes.

The noun that a relative clause refers to may be the subject or object of the verb in the relative clause. In *the bullet that killed him, the bullet* is the subject of the verb *killed*. In *the umbrella that I left on the train, the umbrella* is the object of the verb *left*. Similarly, in *the people who live here, the people* is the subject of the verb *live*. In *the man whom she married, the man* is the object of the verb *married*.

When the noun is the object of a restrictive clause, the relative pronoun (*that* or *whom*) may be omitted:

> the umbrella I left on the train   the man she married
> the clothes they were wearing   this uncle I have never met

But in all other relative clauses – restrictive or non-restrictive – the relative pronoun (*that, which,* or *who*) should not be omitted:

> *the bullet killed him came from this gun
> *my daughter lives in Kent is a doctor

{CONTD}

Which relative pronoun?

The relative pronouns *that* and *which* are used after nouns referring to things. In restrictive clauses you can use *that* or *which*:

> the clothes **that/which** they were wearing
> the umbrella **that/which** I left on the train
> the bullet **that/which** killed him

But in non-restrictive clauses you should use *which*, not *that*:

> this ring, **which** belonged to my grandmother, . . . (not *this ring, **that** belonged to my grandmother)
> Madrid, **which** is the capital of Spain, . . . (not *Madrid, **that** is the capital of Spain, . . .)

The relative pronouns *who* and *whom* are used after nouns referring to people. In formal speech and writing, you use *who* when the noun is the subject of the verb in the relative clause and *whom* when it is the object:

> the people **who** live here   the man **whom** she married

In restrictive clauses you can use *that* instead of *who* or *whom*:

> the people **who/that** live here   my daughter **who/that** lives in Kent
> the man **whom/that** she married   this uncle **whom/that** I have never
> met

But in non-restrictive clauses you should always use *who* or *whom* for people:

> my daughter, **who** lives in Kent (not *my daughter, **that** lives in Kent or *my daughter, **which** lives in Kent)
> this uncle, **whom** I have never met (not *this uncle, **that** I have never met or *this uncle, **which** I have never met)

Finally, when the relative pronoun follows a preposition, you should always use *which* (not *that*) for things and *whom* (not *who*) for people. You cannot say *the paper **in that** it was wrapped or *the person **to who** the letter is addressed.

Sentential relative clauses

A **sentential relative clause** refers back to a whole clause, not just the noun phrase it follows. Sentential relative clauses usually begin with the relative pronoun *which*:

He failed the exam, **which was not surprising**.
She sent me a birthday present, **which was very kind of her**.
I missed the train, **which meant that I was late for my appointment**.
They have not replied, **which suggests that they are not interested**.

Sentential relative clauses may also begin with *for which, in which case*, etc.:

He helped us unload the van, **for which we were very grateful**.
It might rain, **in which case you'll be sorry you chose an open car**.

It is usually quite clear whether a relative clause is sentential or not. But the following sentence is ambiguous:

She was wearing a hat, **which was very unusual**.

Was it the hat that was unusual? Or the fact that she was wearing one? In such cases the ambiguity can only be resolved by rephrasing the sentence.

PEOPLE WHO LIVE IN GLASS HOUSES SHOULDN'T THROW STONES

It is particularly important to distinguish between restrictive and non-restrictive relative clauses when they follow a plural noun. Compare the following two examples:

Journalists **who distort the facts** *are not to be trusted.*
Journalists, **who distort the facts**, *are not to be trusted.*

The first sentence, containing a restrictive relative clause, condemns only those journalists who distort the facts. The second sentence, containing a non-restrictive relative clause, condemns all journalists.
  Here are two more pairs of examples:

French children **who learn English at nursery school** *have a better understanding of language in general.*
French children, **who learn English at nursery school**, *have a better understanding of language in general.*

Do not eat processed foods **which have a high fat content**.
Do not eat processed foods, **which have a high fat content**.

Apposition

When one noun phrase follows another, the phrases are said to be in **apposition**:

Fiona Croft, the society's new
    president

the village policeman, Alan Stone

Canberra, the capital of Australia

Madame Bovary, one of Flaubert's
    best-known works

the subject of the programme,
    drug abuse

Strictly speaking, when phrases are in apposition the order does not matter:

Fiona Croft, the society's new president, made a speech.
The society's new president, Fiona Croft, made a speech.

The subject of the programme, drug abuse, is a topical issue.
Drug abuse, the subject of the programme, is a topical issue.

Similarly, you should be able to remove either of the phrases without changing the meaning of the sentence:

Fiona Croft made a speech.
The society's new president made
    a speech.

The subject of the programme is a
    topical issue.
Drug abuse is a topical issue.

However, the word apposition is also loosely used in other cases:

- when you cannot change the order of the phrases:

  My car, a Renault, is very reliable. (not *A Renault, my car, is very
      reliable.)

- when the second phrase begins with a word or phrase such as *namely*, *for example*, or *that is*:

  her favourite composer, namely Tchaikovsky
  a part of the body, for example the shoulder
  the BBC, that is the British Broadcasting Corporation

Restrictive apposition and non-restrictive apposition

Apposition is usually **non-restrictive**. In other words, you can remove the second phrase without changing the meaning of the sentence.

My car, a Renault, is very reliable. or My car is very reliable.
She is reading a book about her favourite composer, namely Tchaikovsky.

or *She is reading a book about her favourite composer.*

Apposition is occasionally **restrictive**. In other words, the sentence sounds incomplete if you remove the second phrase:

She was taught by the violinist Yehudi Menuhin. not **She was taught by the violinist.* (Which violinist?)
The film Casablanca *is on TV tonight.* not **The film is on TV tonight.* (Which film?)
The word 'desiccate' is often misspelt. not **The word is often misspelt.* (Which word?)

Appositive clauses

An **appositive clause** usually follows an abstract noun such as *fact, idea, thought, belief, decision, suggestion,* etc.:

*the fact **that the reviewer had not seen the film***
*the idea **that computers could take the place of books***

Like a restrictive relative clause, an appositive clause begins with *that*:

*the decision **that was made at the meeting*** (relative clause)
*the decision **that the match should be cancelled*** (appositive clause)

*the suggestion **that you put forward*** (relative clause)
*the suggestion **that he might be innocent*** (appositive clause)

If you find it hard to tell the difference between the two types of clause, try replacing *that* with *which*. This is possible in a relative clause but not in an appositive clause:

*the decision **which** was made at the meeting*
but not **the decision **which** the match should be cancelled*

*the suggestion **which** you put forward*
but not **the suggestion **which** he might be innocent*

Like a phrase in apposition, an appositive clause may be restrictive or non-restrictive:

*She ignored the fact **that the reviewer had not seen the film**.* (restrictive)
*They rejected the suggestion **that he might be innocent**.* (restrictive)
*Their argument, **that the new road layout will increase the number of accidents**, does not hold water.* (non-restrictive)
*This alarming thought – **that he might be guilty** – preyed on her mind.* (non-restrictive)

Adjectives

What is an adjective?

An **adjective** is a word that tells you more about a noun. It tells you what someone or something is like, where someone is from, what something is made of, etc.:

a **good** idea	Her husband is **French**.
the **wooden** box	Paul looks **unhappy**.

Attributive adjectives and predicative adjectives

An **attributive** adjective comes before the noun:

a **good** idea	**German** tourists
my **black** shoes	the **wooden** box

A **predicative** adjective comes after a verb like *be, become, feel, look*, etc. In other words, it is the complement of a copular or linking verb:

The weather was **cold**.	Their offer sounds **tempting**.
This chair is **broken**.	She felt **nervous**.
That smells **delicious**!	Paul looks **unhappy**.

Postpositive adjectives

A **postpositive** adjective comes straight after a pronoun:

somewhere **new**	anything **valuable**
nobody **famous**	everything **possible**

or straight after a noun, especially in fixed phrases:

the heir **apparent**	proof **positive**
time **immemorial**	the village **proper**

The *-ed* form of a verb is often used as a postpositive adjective:

the people **involved**	the tools **required**
the method **used**	everybody **concerned**

Central adjectives and peripheral adjectives

A **central** adjective can be used both attributively and predicatively:

a **huge** dog	The dog was **huge**.
an **interesting** book	That book sounds **interesting**.
bored children	The children look **bored**.

A **peripheral** adjective can be used either attributively or predicatively, but not both. Peripheral adjectives that can only be used attributively include *former, mere, principal, utter,* etc.:

utter incompetence   not *Their incompetence was **utter**.
the **former** president   not *The president is **former**.

Peripheral adjectives that can only be used predicatively include *afraid, alike, alive, asleep,* etc.:

The baby is **asleep**.   not *the **asleep** baby
The flowers look **alike**.   not *the **alike** flowers

Many adjectives are peripheral in some senses only. When *pure* means 'complete' it is a peripheral adjective, but when it means 'unpolluted' it is a central adjective:

pure coincidence   not *The coincidence was **pure**.
pure water   The water is **pure**.

Gradable adjectives and non-gradable adjectives

A **gradable** adjective can be used with words like *very, too, thoroughly, slightly, more/most* (or the endings *-er/-est*), *less/least,* etc.:

a **very expensive** meal   a **more modern** house
We were **slightly disappointed**.   the **funniest** joke I know

Adjectives that cannot be 'graded' in this way are called **non-gradable** adjectives. They include *impossible, perfect, real, supreme,* and *unique.*

THE TIMES THEY ARE A-CHANGIN'

Adjectives that can only be used predicatively often begin with *a-*:

ablaze, adrift, afloat, afoot, afraid, alive, alone, asleep, awake, etc.

The *a-* part of many of these words comes from the Old English preposition *an,* meaning 'on, in, at'. (It is also found in adverbs like *afield, aloud, aside,* etc.) In some literary or old-fashioned texts – and in songs of all ages – you may see *a-* attached to a present participle:

My heart's in the Highlands a-chasing the deer. (Robert Burns)
So, we'll go no more a-roving. (Lord Byron)
Old Time is still a-flying. (Robert Herrick)

{CONTD}

Other uses of adjectives

Adjectives are not always used with a noun or pronoun. They may also

- stand alone as exclamations:

  Wonderful!, Brilliant!, Unbelievable!, Fascinating!, Amazing!

- be used in a **verbless clause**, i.e. a clause in which the verb is omitted:

  *I'd like to catch an earlier train, **if possible**. (= . . . if that is possible)*
  *All our desserts are made with fresh fruit, **when available**. (= . . . when this is available)*

- be used as nouns, usually after *the*:

  *a hostel for **the homeless***   *to attempt **the impossible***
  The poor** are getting poorer and **the   ***The British** fought **the French****
      rich are getting richer.*   *at Waterloo.*

In these examples, the words *homeless, impossible*, etc., are called **nominal adjectives**. Most nominal adjectives refer to people, and they are usually plural. (Exceptions include some *-ed* forms, such as *the accused* or *the deceased*.) Other nominal adjectives are used as abstract nouns, and they are usually singular:

* ***The difficult** we do at once; **the impossible** takes a little longer.*

Order of adjectives

There may be more than one adjective before a noun:

*a **large blue** flower*   *the **old ruined village** church*

These adjectives are sometimes separated by commas:

*a **cool, refreshing** drink*   *a **long, interesting, well-***
*a **dull, rainy** day*   **researched** essay*

There are certain conventions relating to the order of such adjectives. You would not say **a blue large flower* or **the village ruined old church*, for example. These conventions can be summarized as follows:

- first come general adjectives of size, shape, age, temperature, etc.:

  large, small, fat, thin, old, young, new, hot, cold, angry, beautiful

- next come *-ing* forms and *-ed* forms (or irregular equivalents) used as adjectives:

interesting, frightening, isolated, broken

- next come adjectives of colour:

   blue, red, green, yellow, brown, grey

- next come adjectives of nationality, etc.:

   Japanese, Australian, Oriental, Mediterranean

- finally, closest to the noun, come nouns used as adjectives or adjectives derived from nouns:

   garden (in *garden tools*), *village* (in *village church*), *iron, wooden, musical, technological*

Remember that these are conventions, not hard-and-fast rules. The conventional order may be changed for emphasis, as in *an **alarming new development**,* or when one of the adjectives is more closely related to the noun, as in ***Californian red** wine* or *a **surprised old man.***

Adjectives linked by *and, or, but*, etc.

When two or more adjectives are used together they may be linked by *and, or, but,* etc. This usually happens when the adjectives are predicative:

*The inhabitants were **friendly, helpful, and cooperative**.*

*It sounds **exciting but dangerous**.*

But attributive adjectives may also be linked in this way:

*a plant with **blue, yellow, or white** flowers*

*an **interesting but impractical** suggestion*

There are a number of fixed phrases made up of two adjectives linked by *and, or, but,* etc.:

good and ready
right and proper
sweet and sour

cheap and nasty
common or garden
naughty but nice

The adjectives *nice* and *lovely* are often linked to others by *and*:

nice and clean
nice and fresh
nice and early

lovely and warm
lovely and cool
lovely and soft

Making comparisons

You can say that someone or something has more or less of a quality than someone or something else. This is called **comparison**. There are three different kinds of comparison:

- comparison to a higher degree: *Julie is **richer** than Pete.*
- comparison to the same degree: *Pete is **as rich as** Mark.*
- comparison to a lower degree: *Mark is **less rich** than Julie.*

Comparison to a higher degree:
the comparative and the superlative

There are two kinds of comparison to a higher degree:

- the **comparative** form, used to compare two things, people, events, etc.

  *Julie is **richer** than Pete.*　　*You must offer a **more reliable***
  *This is the **nicer** hotel of the two.*　*service than at present.*

- the **superlative** form, used when comparing three or more things, people, events, etc.

  *Julie is the **richest** person I know.*　*This junction is the **most***
  *He was wearing his **oldest** jeans.*　　***dangerous** in the city.*

You form the comparative by adding *-er* to the adjective (*older, smaller*) or by using the word *more* in front of the adjective (***more interesting, more distinctive***). You form the superlative by adding *-est* to the adjective (*oldest, smallest*) or by using the word *most* in front of the adjective (***most interesting, most distinctive***).

The spelling of some adjectives changes when *-er/-est* is added:

- when a single vowel is followed by a single consonant at the end of the adjective, you usually double the consonant before *-er* and *-est*: *wet/wetter/wettest; thin/thinner/thinnest.*

- when the adjective ends in *-y* preceded by a consonant, you usually change the *-y* to *-i-* before *-er* and *-est*: *dry/drier/driest; happy/happier/happiest.* (Note that for adjectives of one syllable the *-y* sometimes does not change. You can use *drier/driest* or *dryer/dryest*, and *spryer* and *spryest* are generally preferred to *sprier* and *spriest*.)

- when the adjective ends in *-e* preceded by a consonant, you drop the *-e* before *-er* and *-est*: *late/later/latest; able/abler/ablest.*

-er/-est or more/most?

Whether you use -er/-est or more/most depends largely on the length of the adjective.

- adjectives of one syllable in length usually add -er/-est: cold/colder/coldest; new/newer/newest; great/greater/greatest. (Note the irregular forms good/better/best; bad/worse/worst.)

- adjectives that are two syllables in length may add -er/-est or take more/most. Those ending in -y usually add -er/-est: angry/angrier/angriest. Some only take more/most: eager/more eager/most eager (not *eagerer/ eagerest). Others may add -er/-est or take more/most: common/commoner/ commonest or common/more common/most common.

- adjectives of three syllables or more usually take more/most: successful/ more successful/most successful. Exceptions include some three-syllable adjectives formed with un-, which add -er/-est: unhappy/unhappier/ unhappiest; unlucky/unluckier/unluckiest.

Comparison to the same degree

Comparison to the same degree is shown by using as before and after the adjective:

> You're **as tall as** your sister.   We're not **as happy as** we were.

Comparison to a lower degree

Comparison to a lower degree is shown by using less or least before the adjective:

> We should help those **less fortunate** than ourselves.
> Yours is the **least attractive** proposal of the three.

WE ARE THE GREATEST!

Comparatives and superlatives are often used in advertising to point out that a particular company's product or service is better than that offered by competitors:

the **easiest** way to pay for your television licence	the very **latest** in technology
a **better** deal on car insurance	how to write a **more effective** CV
one of the **best** collections of Victoriana in the country	the **cheapest** option money can buy
the **widest** range of portable televisions in the High Street	a **more efficient** form of energy
	the **safest** form of contraception
	a **more reliable** delivery service
	the **fastest** scanner available

Other word classes used as adjectives

Adjective or noun?

Nouns are often used as attributive adjectives, before another noun:

the **village** church	a **computer** salesman
milk bottles	her **physics** homework

These are sometimes called **adjectival nouns**. They cannot be used as predicative adjectives, or in comparative or superlative forms:

*The church is **village**.	*a **more village** church
*The bottles are **milk**.	*the **milkest** bottles

However, some adjectival nouns are also adjectives in their own right:

a **French** dictionary (adjectival noun, meaning 'of the French language')
a **French** city (adjective, meaning 'of France')

This may cause ambiguity – *a French teacher* could be either a teacher of the French language or a teacher from France.

Adjective or verb?

The -*ing* and -*ed* forms of verbs can also be used as adjectives:

an **interesting** idea	**faded** jeans
worrying news	an **isolated** spot

These are sometimes called **participial adjectives**, because they have the same form as the present and past participles of the verbs. Irregular equivalents of the -*ed* form are also used in this way:

a **broken** chair	his **swollen** ankle

Unlike adjectival nouns, participial adjectives usually have comparative and superlative forms with *more* and *most*:

a **more interesting** idea	her **most faded** jeans

Also unlike adjectival nouns, participial adjectives can be attributive or predicative:

a **frightening** story	The story was **frightening**.
a **damaged** book	The book is **damaged**.

It is sometimes hard to tell the difference between an *-ing* or *-ed* form used as a predicative adjective and the same word used as the present or past participle of a verb:

> The story was **frightening**.   The story **is frightening** the
>   (adjective)   children. (verb)
> The book is **damaged**. (adjective)   The book **was damaged** in the
>   post. (verb)

Not all adjectives ending in *-ed* or *-ing* are formed from verbs. The *-ed* ending is sometimes added to nouns:

> a *bearded* man   a *dark-haired* child
> a *talented* woman   a *three-legged* stool

And *un-* may be added to participial adjectives to form new adjectives, such as *unsolved, undemanding, unopened, unsurprising, unbroken, unsold.*

Finally, note the difference between *-ing* forms that are participial adjectives and *-ing* forms that are adjectival nouns:

> a *dancing* child (= a child who is dancing)
> a *dancing* teacher (= a teacher of dancing)

Adjective or adverb?

A number of words can be used as adjectives or adverbs:

> a *fast* car (adjective)   to drive *fast* (adverb)
> in *late* summer (adjective)   to work *late* (adverb)

When a word follows the verb *be*, it is sometimes hard to tell whether it is an adjective or an adverb:

> She is **angry**. (adjective)   She is **downstairs**. (adverb)
> My father was **ill**. (adjective)   My father was **abroad**. (adverb)

Generally speaking, if you can replace *be* with a verb like *seem, feel, appear,* or *become,* the word is an adjective:

> She seems angry. (adjective)   not *She seems downstairs.
> My father felt ill. (adjective)   not *My father felt abroad.

Similarly, if you can replace *be* with a verb of action or movement, the word is an adverb:

> She ran downstairs. (adverb)   not *She ran angry.
> My father worked abroad. (adverb)   not *My father worked ill.

Formation of adjectives

New adjectives may be formed in a number of ways. The three most common ways are:

- by adding a fixed ending, called a suffix, to another word:

  drink + -able = drinkable   *care + -less = careless*

- by adding a prefix at the beginning of another adjective:

  dis- + obedient = disobedient   *un- + official = unofficial*

- by joining two or more words together to make a compound adjective:

  sea + sick = seasick   *thread + bare = threadbare*

Suffixes forming adjectives

A **suffix** is a fixed ending that you add to a word (or to part of a word) to form a new word.

- the *suffixes -able, -ant, -atory, -ed, -ent, -ible, -ile, -ing, -ive, -some,* etc., may be added to verbs:

  *drink**able**, prefer**able**; buoy**ant**, resist**ant**; accus**atory**, explor**atory**; cook**ed**, frighten**ed**; absorb**ent**, depend**ent**; convert**ible**, resist**ible**; erect**ile**, tens**ile**; horrify**ing**, interest**ing**; act**ive**, protect**ive**; cuddle**some**, tire**some***

- the suffixes *-al, -an, -ary, -ed, -en, -esque, -ful, -ic, -ine, -ish, -less, -like, -ly, -oid, -ous, -ward, -worthy, -y,* etc., may be added to nouns:

  *herb**al**, magic**al**; Elizabeth**an**, Europe**an**; legend**ary**, revolution**ary**; beard**ed**, hood**ed**; gold**en**, wood**en**; Juno**esque**, pictur**esque**; care**ful**, success**ful**; hero**ic**, rhythm**ic**; alp**ine**, crystall**ine**; child**ish**, fool**ish**; fear**less**, hope**less**; child**like**, war**like**; mother**ly**, saint**ly**; cub**oid**, spher**oid**; danger**ous**, fam**ous**; east**ward**, home**ward**; blame**worthy**, news**worthy**; health**y**, oil**y***

- the suffixes *-er, -est, -ish, -most,* etc., may be added to other adjectives:

  *old**er**, small**er**; great**est**, new**est**; green**ish**, young**ish**; hind**most**, upper**most***

Note that words ending in *-e* drop this letter before some suffixes:

  explore → exploratory   *scare → scared*
  picture → picturesque   *large → largest*

surprise → surprising	cube → cuboid
fame → famous	

Before the suffix -able, the -*e* is usually dropped:

admire → admirable not *admireable   use → usable not *useable

But note that *manageable, replaceable*, etc., keep the -*e*- to stop the 'soft' sound of the -*g*- and -*c*- changing to the 'hard' sound of *gable* and *cable*.

Some other -*able* words have two possible spellings:

like → likable or likeable   size → sizable or sizeable

Sometimes other letters are dropped, added, or changed:

rely → reliable, reliant	circle → circular
knit → knitted	neglect → negligible
permit → permissible	crystal → crystalline

Prefixes

A **prefix** is a fixed group of letters that you add at the beginning of a word to form another word, usually with a different meaning.

The prefixes *dis-, il-, im-, in-, ir-, non-, un-* give an adjective the opposite meaning:

disagreeable, **dis**obedient; **il**legitimate, **il**literate; **im**patient, **im**possible; **in**convenient, **in**credible; **non**-resident, **non**-violent; **un**able, **un**official

Note that *non-* also combines with verbs to form adjectives:

a **non-iron** shirt	a **non-stick** pan
a **non-return** valve	a **non-slip** surface
a **non-stop** flight	

Other prefixes include:

anti- **anti**malarial, **anti**social	micro- **micro**analytical,
hyper- **hyper**critical,	**micro**photographic
hypersensitive	over- **over**indulgent, **over**productive
inter- **inter**dependent,	super- **super**conductive,
international	**super**natural

You will find more information about prefixes and suffixes in the section 'Formation of nouns' on page 68.

{CONTD}

Compound adjectives

A **compound adjective** is made up of two or more other words. They are usually linked by a hyphen – often to avoid ambiguity when they come before the noun. Some of the more common ones are written as one word (e.g. *seasick, threadbare*) and others may be written as two words when they come after the noun.

Here are some of the most frequent types of compound adjective:

- noun + adjective:

  water-resistant clothing, an *ozone-friendly* aerosol, *duty-free* goods, a *top-heavy* load, *paper-thin* slices, a *work-shy* teenager, *computer-mad* children, a *heatproof* dish, a *threadbare* carpet

- noun + *-ing* form of verb:

  the *car-owning* majority, a *German-speaking* editor, a *soul-destroying* experience, a *heart-rending* cry, a *mind-boggling* idea, an *ear-splitting* noise, of *child-bearing* age, the *cinema-going* public

- noun + past participle:

  home-made clothes, *shop-bought* cakes, her *grief-stricken* father, an *oil-based* fuel, *snow-covered* hills

- adjective (or determiner) + noun + *-ed*:

  a *red-haired* child, a *three-legged* dog, a *many-sided* personality, a *right-angled* triangle, their *whole-hearted* support

- compound noun (or adjective + noun) used adjectivally:

  a *chocolate-box* village, a *low-profile* approach, a *swimming-pool* attendant

- numeral + noun used adjectivally:

  a *five-mile* walk, a *three-year* contract, a *first-class* ticket, a *second-rate* performance, a *nineteenth-century* politician

- *ill-* or *well-* + past participle:

  an *ill-founded* rumour, a *well-written* essay, an *ill-bred* person, a *well-known* composer, an *ill-behaved* child

- past participle + adverb:

  a *broken-down* car, *worn-out* shoes

- duplicated adjectives:

  a **pretty-pretty** design, her **clever-clever** ideas, his **goody-goody** behaviour, a **teeny-weeny** slice

- other combinations:

  bitter-sweet memories, a **black-and-white** photograph, an **across-the-board** payment, **state-of-the-art** equipment, a **devil-may-care** attitude

Compound adjectives of colour

There are many compound adjectives of colour, such as *off-white*, *shocking pink*, *pitch black*, *lime green*, *navy blue*, *Titian red*.

Some mean 'as . . . as . . .', such as *snow white* (= as white as snow), *pitch black*, *jet black*, *coal black*, *sloe black*.

Many noun + colour combinations denote a particular shade of the colour, such as *salmon pink* (= of the pink colour of a salmon), *emerald green*, *sky blue*, *cherry red*, *canary yellow*, *charcoal grey*, *chocolate brown*. Some do not mention a specific colour, simply adding *-coloured* to the noun: *rust-coloured*, *coffee-coloured*, *flesh-coloured*, *rose-coloured*, etc.

There are a wide range of compounds denoting a shade between two colours, such as *blue-black*, *silver-grey*, *yellow-brown*, *orange-pink*, *purple-red*, *blue-green*. Then there are the *-ish* compounds: *reddish-yellow*, *yellowish-red*, *greenish-blue*, *greyish-brown*, etc.

Finally, the colour adjective may simply be preceded by *light*, *dark*, *pale*, *bright*, etc., as in *light blue*, *dark green*, *pale pink*, *bright yellow*.

USER-FRIENDLY COMPUTERS FOR TECHNOLOGICALLY CHALLENGED PEOPLE

The compound adjective *user-friendly* was coined in the 1970s as a computing term and became a buzzword of the 1980s. Advertisers, journalists, and other writers seized on the *-friendly* part of the adjective, and soon we had *environment-friendly detergents*, *ozone-friendly aerosols*, *reader-friendly documents*, *dolphin-friendly tuna*, etc.

A few years later, it was the politically correct term *challenged* that caught the public imagination. The adjective phrase *physically challenged*, used euphemistically in place of *disabled*, led to a host of facetious new coinages: *vertically challenged* (i.e. small), *socially challenged*, *financially challenged*, *technologically challenged*, etc.

The adjective phrase

An adjective may be used with other words that tell you more about it:

very warm   fond **of children**
deeply shocked   reluctant **to help**
cold **enough**   stronger **than usual**

This group of words, including the adjective, is called an **adjective phrase**. The adjective itself – *warm, shocked, cold, fond, reluctant, stronger* – is called the **head adjective**. As in a noun phrase, the words used before the head adjective are called **premodifiers**, and the words used after the head adjective are called **postmodifiers**.

Premodifiers of the head adjective

The head adjective often has an adverb in front of it:

a **very** warm day   The soup is **too** salty.
The issue is **extremely** complex.   a **rather** old joke
a **surprisingly** comfortable chair   It's **quite** possible.
I was **deeply** shocked.   a **freshly** ironed shirt
a **fairly** common problem   This is **morally** unacceptable.

Sometimes more than one adverb is used:

He is **almost too** enthusiastic.   These glasses are **very easily** broken.

The head adjective occasionally has another adjective in front:

a **great** big box   Her hair was **dark** brown.
a **tiny** little snail   The carpet is **pale** green.

Sometimes the adjective is repeated:

a **long long** time   The water got **deeper and deeper**.
big big trouble   He became **fatter and fatter**.

An adjective phrase that consists simply of adverb + adjective may be used attributively (before the noun):

a **very warm** day   a **rather old** joke
a **surprisingly comfortable** chair   a **freshly ironed** shirt
a **fairly common** problem

or predicatively (after the verb *be*, etc.):

> The issue is **extremely complex**. It's **quite possible**.
> I was **deeply shocked**. This is **morally unacceptable**.
> The soup is **too salty**.

Postmodifiers of the head adjective

The head adjective may be followed by

- an adverb: *cold enough*
- a phrase beginning with a preposition: *fond of animals; pleased with the response*
- a clause beginning with an infinitive: *reluctant to help; easy to clean*
- a clause beginning with an *-ing* form: *busy looking for a new house; happy playing in the sand*
- a clause beginning with a *wh*-word: *sure what to do; uncertain where to start looking*
- a clause beginning with *than*: *stronger than usual; harder than it looks*
- a clause beginning with *that*: *confident that he would win; glad (that) you like it*
- a combination of these: *good enough to eat* (adverb + infinitive clause); *fonder than ever of the children* (*than*-clause + prepositional phrase)

When the head adjective has a postmodifier or postmodifiers, it is usually in a predicative position:

> The wine is not **cold enough**. I'm not **sure where she lives**.
> He is **fond of animals**. The coffee tastes **stronger than**
> We were **pleased with the response**. **usual**.
> She seemed **reluctant to help**. He was **confident that he would**
> They are **busy looking for a new** **win**.
>   house. That looks **good enough to eat!**

More complex adjective phrases

More complex adjective phrases may have premodifiers *and* postmodifiers:

> I was **extremely glad of your** She is **too ready to criticize**.
>   advice. We are **more determined than**
> He was **very lucky indeed**. **ever**.

Pronouns

What is a pronoun?

A **pronoun** is a word that you use instead of a noun:

you, it, that, who, everything, somebody, one

You often use a pronoun to avoid repeating a noun or noun phrase:

*Caroline phoned William and told **him** [= William] the news.*
*The caretaker closed the door and locked **it** [= the door].*

You can also use a pronoun in place of a clause:

*He destroyed all her letters. – Why did he do **that**?*
*I managed to persuade them, but **it** wasn't easy.*

In all the above examples, the pronoun refers back to something already mentioned. This is not always the case. The pronoun may refer to something unknown or unspecified:

*Can you see **anything**?*   ***Somebody** has broken my*
*He copies **everything** I do.*   *favourite vase.*

Sometimes you indicate the person or thing you mean by pointing, etc.:

*What is **this** for?*   *How much are **those**?*

In a clause or sentence, pronouns usually behave like nouns. In other words, they may be the subject, object, or complement of a verb:

I have never been to Australia. (subject)
*He picked up the book and put **it** on the table.* (direct object)
*Give **her** another chance.* (indirect object)
*These shoes must be **yours**.* (complement)

They may also follow a preposition:

*These flowers are for **you**.*   *He arrived in one car and left in*
*The envelope had her name on **it**.*   ***another**.*

Types of pronoun

There are a number of different types of pronoun. They include

- personal pronouns: *I, me, you, he, him, she, her, it, we, us, they, them*

  *I love **him**.*   *There are two letters for **you**.*

- reflexive pronouns: *myself, yourself, ourselves, themselves*, etc.

  She blamed **herself**.   They kept the best for **themselves**.

- possessives: *my, mine, your, yours, his, her, hers, its, our, ours, their, theirs*

  Where are **my** car keys?   These books are **ours**.

- demonstratives: *this, that, these, those*

  That smells good!   What should I do with **these**?

- interrogatives: *what, which, who, whom, whose*

  Which do you want?   **Whose** is this scarf?

- relative pronouns: *that, which, who, whom, whose*

  the book **that** I am reading   the people **who** live here

- reciprocal pronouns: *each other, one another*

  The children hate **each other**.   We must help **one another**.

- indefinite pronouns: *everything, somebody, anyone, nothing, nobody, all, some, each, both, none, either*, etc.

  Nobody replied.   **Some** were damaged.

IT NEVER RAINS BUT IT POURS!

The pronoun *it* has a wide range of uses:

- as a personal pronoun

I dropped the vase and broke it.   *I patted the dog and **it** bit me.*

- referring to time, weather, etc.

It *is nearly midnight.*   **It's** *cold outside.*
It's *Tuesday tomorrow.*   **It** *snowed all night.*

- referring to a clause at the end of the sentence

It's *a pity he can't come.*   **It** *doesn't matter what you wear.*
It *seems unlikely that they will*   **It** *can't be easy, bringing up four*
    change their mind.   *children on your own.*

- in idiomatic phrases

*I take **it** you don't mind.*   *How's **it** going?*
*You've had **it**!*   *They were having **it** off on the sofa.*

Personal pronouns

The **personal pronouns** are *I, me, you, he, him, she, her, it, we, us, they,* and *them*. Most of them are chiefly used in place of nouns that refer to people:

Sally lives next door to Jack. → ***She** lives next door to **him**.*

The personal pronouns *it* and *they* are exceptions. You use *it* for nouns that refer to animals or things, and *they* for all plural nouns.

Person, number, gender, and case

Personal pronouns change their form according to person (e.g. *I/you*), number (e.g. *it/they*), gender (e.g. *he/she*), and case (e.g. *I/me*).

- the **first person** (*I, me, we, us*) is or includes the person who is talking:

    ***I** bent down to pat the dog and it bit **me**.*
    ***Chris and I** went to the cinema but **we** didn't enjoy the film: it scared **us**.*

- the **second person** (*you*) is the person or people you are talking to:

    *If **you** don't hurry up, I'll go without **you**.*
    ***Peter and Neil**, where are **you** going with that bucket of water?*

- the **third person** (*he, him, she, her, it, they, them*) is the person, people, or thing(s) you are talking about:

    *We invited **Michael**, but **he** couldn't come.*
    *I bought **these apples** because they were cheaper, but I don't like
    them.*

The **number** of a personal pronoun may be singular or plural:
- first person singular: *I, me*
- first person plural: *we, us*
- second person singular: *you*
- second person plural: *you*
- third person singular: *he, him, she, her, it*
- third person plural: *they, them*

The **gender** of a personal pronoun may be masculine or feminine. Only the third person singular changes according to gender:

*My brother runs a shop. **He** often has to work at the weekend – I
    don't envy **him**! (masculine)*
*My sister is a company director. **She** is often away on business, so I
    don't see **her** very often. (feminine)*

Personal pronouns also change according to **case**. When the pronoun is the subject of a verb it is in the subjective case (*I, you, he, she, it, we, they*):

I like chocolate.   *My car has a flat battery and **it***
*What do **you** want?*   *won't start.*

When the pronoun is the object of a verb, or when it follows a preposition, it is in the objective case (*me, you, him, her, it, us, them*):

*My parents helped **me**.*   *Give **it** to **her**.*
*This letter is for **you**.*   *Tell **him** what to do.*

When a personal pronoun is in the genitive case, showing possession, it is usually known as a possessive: ***my** car, **your** hat, **his** fault, **her** idea, **its** nest, **our** friends, **their** pets*

You will find more information about the gender of pronouns on page 126, the case of pronouns on page 128, and possessives on page 118.

Other uses of *you*, *one*, and *they*

You can also use the personal pronoun *you*, and its possessive and reflexive forms *your, yours, yourself*, to refer to people in general:

*In a self-service shop **you** help **yourself**.*
*It is easy to lose **your** way in the winding streets of the town.*

In some formal contexts *one* may be used instead:

*In a self-service shop **one** helps **oneself**.*
*It is easy to lose **one's** way in the winding streets of the town.*

This usage is rather old-fashioned, and *you* is increasingly used in place of *one*. Note that the possessive form *one's* has an apostrophe, unlike *its*. Note also that *you* is still used with a verb in the second person singular, and *one* with a verb in the third person singular, even though both words mean 'people in general': *you **help*** but *one **helps***.

You can also use the personal pronoun *they* to refer to people in general, or to a vague or unspecified group of people:

***They** say that swimming is one of the best forms of exercise.*
*Do you think **they** are likely to raise interest rates again this year?*

Reflexive pronouns

The reflexive pronouns have the ending -*self* (in the singular) or -*selves* (in the plural):

> my**self**, your**self**, him**self**, her**self**, it**self**, one**self**, our**selves**, your**selves**, them**selves**

They usually refer back to a noun or pronoun mentioned earlier. This earlier noun or pronoun is often the subject of the clause or sentence.

I blamed **myself**.	*It* switches **itself** off.
You must wash **yourself**.	**We** congratulated **ourselves**.
My brother went by **himself**.	**You** shouldn't demean **yourselves**.
Mary's talking to **herself**.	**The children** helped **themselves**.

Person, number, and gender

Like the personal pronouns, reflexive pronouns change their form according to person, number (singular or plural), and gender (masculine or feminine):

- first person singular: *myself*
- second person singular: *yourself*
- third person singular: *himself herself, itself*
- first person plural: *ourselves*
- second person plural: *yourselves*
- third person plural: *themselves*

Uses of the reflexive pronoun

A reflexive pronoun may be used:

- as the direct object of a verb

  *I blamed **myself** for the death of the child.*
  *She prides **herself** on her objectivity.*
  *The dog stood up and scratched **itself**.*
  *We washed **ourselves** in a mountain stream.*
  *You'll kick **yourselves** when I tell you!*
  *They absented **themselves** from the meeting.*

- as the indirect object of a verb:

  *I bought **myself** a cup of coffee as a reward.*
  *You'll give **yourself** a headache trying to read that small print.*
  *He told **himself** it didn't matter what happened.*

- after a preposition:

  *She was angry with **herself** for forgetting the key.*
  *They kept the best wine for **themselves**.*

- for emphasis:

  *I **myself** prefer classical music to jazz.*
  *The suspect's name was not mentioned in the article **itself**.*

In standard English the reflexive pronoun has to 'reflect' another word:

*I bought some food for Jane and **myself**.* (*myself* 'reflects' the pronoun *I*)
***Peter** bought some food for Jane and **himself**.* (*himself* 'reflects' the
  noun *Peter*)

It should not be used in place of the personal pronoun:

*Jane and **I** went to the cinema.* (not **Jane and **myself** went to the
  cinema.*)
*Peter was hungry, so I bought some food for Jane and **him**.* (not **Peter
  was hungry, so I bought some food for Jane and **himself**.*)

In the last example, *himself* cannot be used to 'reflect' the noun *Peter*
because it is in a different clause. *Peter* is not the subject of the verb *bought*.

If you are ever in doubt about which pronoun to use in a noun phrase
containing *and*, *or*, etc., try removing the rest of the phrase:

*[Jane and] **I** went to the cinema.* (not *****Myself** went to the cinema.*)

I'M NOT FEELING MYSELF

Reflexive pronouns are used in a number of idiomatic phrases:

*They were **beside themselves** with worry.* (i.e. overwhelmed)
*She is getting a bit **above herself**.* (i.e. arrogant)
*He **wasn't himself** yesterday.* (i.e. not his usual self)
*She **forgot herself** and began to dance wildly to the music.* (i.e. failed to behave
  with her usual dignity)
*Did you **enjoy yourselves**?* (i.e. have a good time)
*Do you like living **by yourself**?* (i.e. on your own)
*I built this house **all by myself**.* (i.e. without help from others)
*We had the swimming pool **(all) to ourselves**.* (i.e. nobody else was there)

Possessives

The **possessives** are the set of words that show personal possession:

my, mine, your, yours, his, her, hers, its, our, ours, their, theirs

They may be divided into two groups:

- those that are used as pronouns (*mine, yours, his, hers, ours, theirs*):

  *This book is **mine**.*
  I haven't brought a pen – may I
      *borrow **yours**?*
  *Which is **hers**?*

  *This isn't Jack's mug – **his** has a*
      broken handle.
  ***Ours** are red and **theirs** are blue.*

- those that behave like adjectives, and are called determiners (*my, your, his, her, its, our, their*):

  *This is **my** book.*
  *May I borrow **your** pen?*
  *What does **her** job involve?*
  ***His** mug has a broken handle.*

  *The dog was chasing **its** tail.*
  ***Our** children are at school.*
  ***Their** names are James and Isabel.*

Some grammar books and dictionaries call both groups *possessive pronouns*. Others treat them separately, as pronouns and determiners. Some call the determiners *possessive adjectives*.

Person, number, and gender

Like the personal pronouns, possessives change their form according to person, number (singular or plural), and gender (masculine or feminine):

- first person singular: *my, mine*
- second person singular: *your, yours*
- third person singular: *his, her, its, his, hers*

- first person plural: *our, ours*
- second person plural: *your, yours*
- third person plural: *their, theirs*

Note that unlike possessives in some other languages, the words *my, your,* etc., do not change their form before plural nouns:

*I can't find **my scarf** or **my gloves**.*
*This is **his brother** and these are **his sisters**.*

Nor do *mine, yours,* etc., change their form when they replace a plural noun:

*That scarf is **yours**. / Those gloves are **yours**.*

The possessive also stays the same whether it is used as the subject, object, complement, or after a preposition:

***Mine** has a broken handle.*
(subject)
*You can borrow **mine**.* (object)
*This is **mine**.* (complement)
*I towed their boat behind **mine**.*
(after preposition)

***Our** house has double glazing.*
(subject)
*You can borrow **our** car.* (object)
*This is **our** dog.* (complement)
*We towed the dinghy behind **our** yacht.* (after preposition)

Uses of the possessive

You can use a possessive instead of a noun in the genitive case (i.e. a noun with *'s*):

*She bought **Paul's** car.* → *She bought **his** car.*
*Where are **the children's** parents?* → *Where are **their** parents?*
*These are my boots; those are **Suzanne's**.* → *These are my boots; those are **hers**.*
*I've found your jacket, but I can't find **your brother's**.* → *I've found your jacket, but I can't find **his**.*

You can also use the possessives *mine, yours, his, hers, ours,* and *theirs* in place of a noun preceded by *my, your,* etc.:

*This must be your hat: **mine** [= **my hat**] is red.*
*I haven't brought a pen – may I borrow **yours** [= **your pen**]?*
*Whose bag is this? It is **hers** [= **her bag**].*
*Their house is smaller than **ours** [= **our house**].*

Note that there is no apostrophe before the final *-s* of the possessives *yours, hers, its, ours, theirs:*

*The accident was nobody's fault but **yours** [not ***your's**].*
*These shoes must be **hers** [not ***her's**].*
*The dog wagged **its** [not ***it's**] tail.*
***Ours** [not ***Our's**] was more expensive.*
*You can use **theirs** [not ***their's**].*

However, the possessive *one's* does have an apostrophe:

*It is easy to lose **one's** [not ***ones**] way in the winding streets of the town.*

The word *it's* (with an apostrophe) is short for *it is* or *it has*, and should not be confused with the possessive *its:*

***It's** raining again.* (= ***It is** raining again.*)
***It's** fallen over.* (= ***It has** fallen over.*)
*Look at the cat: **it's** eaten **its** dinner and now **it's** licking **its** paws.*

Other types of pronoun

Demonstratives

The **demonstratives** are the set of words *this, that, these,* and *those. These* is the plural of *this,* and *those* is the plural of *that.* They are used to point out or distinguish between people or things. You generally use *this* and *these* when the person or thing is close to you and *that* or *those* when they are further away.

> **This** book is more expensive than **that** one.
> **That** is your bed; **this** is mine.
> **Those** banknotes are worthless but **these** old coins are very valuable.
> **These** are my children; **those** are their friends.

Like the possessives, the demonstratives may be used as determiners or pronouns. When they are used as determiners (i.e. before a noun) they are sometimes called *demonstrative adjectives.* Unlike the possessives, the demonstratives have the same form for both uses:

> *Whose is **this** pen?* (determiner)　　*Whose is **this**?* (pronoun)
> *You can't go to the party in **those**　You can't go to the party in
> shoes!* (determiner)　　　　　　　　**those**! (pronoun)

Interrogatives

The **interrogatives** are a set of pronouns and determiners that are used to ask questions: *what, which, who, whom,* and *whose.* (You can also use words like *how, when, where,* and *why* to ask questions. These are **interrogative adverbs.**) Because most of these words (except *how*) begin with *wh-,* they are sometimes called *wh-***words.**

Using *what* and *which*

You can use the interrogatives *what* and *which* as pronouns or determiners:

> **What** *does she want?* (pronoun)　　**Which** *does she want?* (pronoun)
> **What** *film did you see?* (determiner)　**Which** *film did you see?*
> 　　　　　　　　　　　　　　　　　　(determiner)

The interrogative pronoun *what* means 'what thing'. It usually refers to an indefinite or unlimited range of items. The interrogative pronoun *which,* on the other hand, refers to a more definite or limited choice.

The answer to the question *What does she want?* could be almost anything, such as *something to eat,* a *job,* £500, *a new car, some assistance,* etc.

The answer to the question *Which does she want?* will be one of the range of items that she has been offered, such as *the blue one, the Ferrari, a glass of wine,* etc.

Similarly, when *what* and *which* are determiners, *what film* may refer to all the films on general release and *which film* may refer to the three or four films currently showing at the local cinema.

Both *what* and *which* may be the subject or object of the verb:

What is making that noise? (subject)

Which shall we buy? (object)

Which students are most likely to fail? (subject)

What reasons did they give? (object)

You can use the determiners *what* and *which* before any type of noun, singular or plural, referring to people, animals, or things:

What mother would risk her child's life?

What bird lays eggs as big as this?

What reasons did they give?

Which assistant served you?

Which mammals live in the sea?

Which shoes should I wear?

You can also use the pronoun *which* in place of any type of noun. But the pronoun *what* is not used in place of nouns referring to people – *who* or *whom* is used instead.

Using *who, whom,* and *whose*

The interrogative *who* is used only as a pronoun, meaning 'what or which person or people'. It is usually the subject of the verb:

Who is in charge?

Who broke this window?

Who are the best players in the club?

The interrogative *whom* is also used only as a pronoun, meaning 'what or which person or people'. It is never the subject of the verb, but is used as the object or after a preposition in formal English:

Whom did they choose?

To **whom** should I address the letter?

In informal English *who* is often used instead of *whom*:

Who did they choose?

Who should I address the letter to?

The interrogative *whose* may be a pronoun or determiner. It is the possessive form of *who/whom*:

Whose are these? (pronoun)

Whose fault is it? (determiner)

{CONTD}

Relative pronouns

The **relative pronouns** *that*, *which*, *who*, *whom*, and *whose* are used at the beginning of a relative clause, which comes after a noun and tells you more about it:

> the clothes **that** they were wearing
> this ring, **which** belonged to my
> grandmother, . . .

> Peter, **who** is an accountant, . . .
> the child **whose** bag had been
> stolen

(You can also use words like *when* and *where* at the beginning of a relative clause. These are **relative adverbs**.)

Which, *whom*, and *whose* are sometimes used with a preposition in front:

> the paper **in which** it was wrapped
> the person **to whom** the letter is
> addressed

> the man **with whom** she arrived
> the students **for whose** benefit
> the lecture was given

Note that the relative pronoun *whose* is really a determiner – it always comes before a noun: *the child **whose bag** had been stolen; the students for **whose benefit** the lecture was given.*

The relative pronoun *which* may also be a determiner:

> the piano, **which instrument** he has played since childhood
> computer graphics, **on which subject** she is an expert

Which relative pronoun?

Who and *whom* are used after nouns referring to people. In formal speech and writing, *who* is used when the noun is the subject of the verb in the relative clause and *whom* when it is the object.

> the people **who** live here

> the man **whom** she married

Whose is used after nouns referring to people, animals, or things:

> the child **whose** bag had been stolen

> the cat **whose** kitten I bought

That and *which* are chiefly used after nouns referring to animals or things, but *that* can also be used after nouns referring to people.

In some relative clauses you can use *that* or *which*:

> the clothes **that/which** they were wearing
> the umbrella **that/which** I left on the train

In some relative clauses you can use *that* instead of *who* or *whom*:

*the people **who/that** live here*   *the man **whom/that** she married*

You will find more information about relative clauses on pages 88–91.

Reciprocal pronouns

The **reciprocal pronouns** are *each other* and *one another*. You use them to show a mutual or two-way action or relationship:

*The children hate **each other**.*   *We must help **one another**.*
*We looked at **each other** and smiled.*   *They bought gifts for **one another**.*

A reciprocal pronoun is always used with a plural subject:

***The children** hate **each other**.*   ***We** must help **one another**.*

It may be the object of a verb:

*The children **hate each other**.*   *We must **help one another**.*

or it may follow a preposition:

*We looked **at each other** and*
*   smiled.*

*They bought gifts **for one**
*   **another**.*

Reciprocal pronouns usually refer to people or animals, but they can also refer to things:

*The two surfaces rub against **each other** to produce a spark.*
*The cars followed **one another** around the circuit.*

LOVE ONE ANOTHER

There is a traditional 'rule' that you should only use *each other* for two people, animals or things. If three or more items are involved, you should use *one another* instead.

This rule, according to H. W. Fowler in *A Dictionary of Modern English Usage*, is 'neither of present utility nor based on historical usage'. It is frequently disregarded by the great and the good:

. . . all his men / Looked at **each other** with a wild surmise . . . (John Keats, 'On
   First Looking into Chapman's Homer')
It was very good of God to let Carlyle and Mrs Carlyle marry **one another** and so
   make only two people miserable instead of four. (Samuel Butler, *Letters*)

{CONTD}

Indefinite pronouns

The **indefinite pronouns** fall into two main groups:

- the compound pronouns:

  everything, everybody, everyone; something, somebody, someone;
  anything, anybody, anyone; nothing, nobody, no one

(Note that the -*where* compounds *everywhere, somewhere, anywhere*, and *nowhere* are adverbs, not pronouns.)

- pronouns that may be followed by *of*, such as:

  all, some, each, both, one, none, either, neither, another, much, many,
  more, most, (a) few, fewer, fewest, (a) little, less, least, etc.

Compound pronouns

The compound pronouns may be used as the subject or object of a verb, or after a preposition:

> **Nobody** objected to the proposal. (subject)
> He doesn't want **anything**. (direct object)
> She bought **everyone** a present. (indirect object)
> Are you looking for **something**? (after preposition)

When a compound pronoun is the subject, the verb is always singular, even if the pronoun seems to refer to more than one person or thing:

> **Everybody receives** the same   **Is anything** missing?
>   amount of money.   **Something** always **goes** wrong.
> **No one was** allowed to leave early.

Pronouns that may be followed by of

These are mainly expressions of quantity – *all, some, both*, etc. Most of them (except *none*) are also used as determiners. As pronouns, all of them can be followed by *of*:

> **Some** were destroyed.   **Some of** them were destroyed.
> **Some of** the books were destroyed.

The indefinite pronouns *all, some, none, more*, and *most* may be singular or plural. They are singular when they are used with or instead of a singular noun or an uncountable noun (i.e. a noun that cannot be made plural). They are plural when they are used with or instead of a plural noun:

Most (of the lake) **was** frozen. (singular)
All (of the eggs) **were** broken. (plural)

The pronouns *each, either, neither,* and *another* are only used with or instead of plural nouns. But the pronoun is always singular, because it refers to only one of the people or things:

Each (of the suspects) **has** an alibi. **Another** (of the houses) **was** sold
Neither (of the lifts) **is** working. last month.

Both, many, (a) few, fewer, and *fewest* are only used with or instead of plural nouns. But these pronouns refer to more than one of the people or things, so they are always plural:

Both (of the suspects) **have** an **Many** (of the houses) **were** sold
  alibi. last month.

Much, (a) little, less, and *least* are always singular. They are most often used with or instead of an uncountable noun:

Much (of the money) **has** been spent. **Little** (of the wine) **remains**.
Much (of the lake) **was** frozen. **Little** (of the article) **is** true.

The pronoun *one*

The pronoun *one* is used in a variety of ways:

- as an indefinite pronoun:

  *I have two sisters: **one** is a teacher and the other (**one**) is a lawyer.*

- with an adjective or a determiner:

  *There are three cars outside: a red **one**, a black **one**, and a blue **one**.*

- with *each, either, neither, another,* etc.:

  *Either (**one**) will do.* *Would you like another (**one**)?*

- in the plural form *ones*:

  *Those are my old shoes; these are the **ones** I bought yesterday.*
  *Don't use the dirty cups – there are some clean **ones** in the cupboard.*

- as a personal pronoun in formal or old-fashioned English:

  ***One** sometimes sees deer in these woods.*
  *It pays **one** to shop around for insurance.*
  *It is easy to lose **one's** way in the winding streets of the town.*

Gender of pronouns

The **gender** of a word tells you whether it is masculine or feminine. The only pronouns that change according to gender are the third person singular of the personal pronoun (and related words):

he, him, himself, his; she, her, herself, hers; it, itself, its

- the pronouns *he, him, himself,* and *his* are used for masculine nouns, i.e. those referring to male people and (some) male animals:

  *I asked **my son** but **he** didn't know.*   *Don't forget to give **the dog his**
  *There's **Mike** – can you see **him**?*   *dinner.*
  ***The boy** fell and hurt **himself**.*   *Ask **Mr Jones** if this book is **his**.*

- the pronouns *she, her, herself,* and *hers* are used for feminine nouns, i.e. those referring to female people and (some) female animals:

  *There's **Kate** – can you see **her**?*   ***The cow** looked around for **her**
                                                calf.
  ***The girl** fell and hurt **herself**.*   *Ask **Mrs Jones** if this book is **hers**.*

You can also use these pronouns for boats and ships (and sometimes for cars and other vehicles), or for countries:

  *If the **boat** capsizes **she** will right*   ***Greece** has increased **her** exports.*
  ***herself**.*

- the pronouns *it, itself,* and *its* are used for all other nouns:

  *This is **an unconventional method**, but **it** works.*
  *They put **their house** on the market and sold **it** within a month.*

You can also use these pronouns for babies and young children, especially if the sex is not known or not relevant:

  ***A baby** soon learns to recognize **its** parents.*
  ***The child of a broken marriage** may blame **itself** for what happened.*

Dual gender

You can use a pronoun of **dual gender** for both masculine and feminine nouns. In other words, it refers to people of either sex.

The pronouns *they, them, themselves, their,* and *theirs* are plural pronouns of dual gender. Unfortunately, there is no singular equivalent in the English language, apart from the phrases *he or she, his or her,* etc.

Problems arise when you want to use a personal pronoun with a word like *everybody, someone, anyone,* or *nobody,* or with a phrase like *each applicant, the winner, one of the passengers, any person,* etc. You do not know the sex of the person, so you need a singular pronoun of dual gender. There are a number of possibilities:

• the phrases *he or she, him or her, himself or herself, his or her,* etc., are the most 'correct' options, but they sound rather clumsy:

> If anyone disagrees, **he or she** will be given the opportunity to say so.
> If anybody calls, tell **him or her** to ring back later.
> The culprit was encouraged to give **him or herself** up to the police.
> The student is expected to provide **his or her** own books and stationery.

• the traditional solution was to use the masculine pronouns *he, him, himself,* and *his* as pronouns of dual gender:

> If anyone disagrees, **he** will be given the opportunity to say so.
> If anybody calls, tell **him** to ring back later.
> The culprit was encouraged to give **himself** up to the police.
> The student is expected to provide **his** own books and stationery.

But this does not work, because it sounds as though you are only talking about men, not women.

• in modern English you will often find the pronouns *they, them,* etc. used instead, especially with words like *everybody, someone,* etc.:

> If anyone disagrees, **they** will be given the opportunity to say so.
> If anybody calls, tell **them** to ring back later.
> Nobody should blame **themselves** for what happened.
> We gave everyone **their** money back.

• in some cases, it may be simpler to make the problematic phrase plural:

> **The students** are expected to provide **their** own books and stationery.

You will find more information about gender in the section 'Gender of nouns' on page 64.

HIS AND HERS

There have been many attempts to 'invent' a singular pronoun of dual gender: *s/he, hesh, hir, co, tey, thon, heesh,* etc. Of these, only *s/he* has found its way into occasional use.

Case of pronouns

In Latin and some other languages, pronouns have different forms for use as the subject, object, etc. This fixed pattern of changes is called the **case** system. In English, only a small number of pronouns change their form according to case.

Some have different forms for the **genitive case**, showing possession:

> *I → my/mine, you → your/yours, he → his, she → her/hers, etc.; who → whose*

Some have different forms for use as the subject of a verb (the **subjective case**) and for use as the object of a verb or after a preposition (the **objective case**).

> *I → me, he → him, she → her, we → us, they → them; who → whom*

The genitive case

The pronouns that change their form for the genitive case (to show possession) are:

- the personal pronouns *I, you, he, she, it, we,* and *they,* which change to the possessives *my, mine; your, yours; his; her, hers; its; our, ours;* and *their, theirs*:

> *I have a car; it is **my** car; it is **mine**.*
> *You have a bike; it is **your** bike; it is **yours**.*
> *He has a house; it is **his** house; it is **his**.*
> *She has a dog; it is **her** dog; it is **hers**.*
> *It has a tail; this is **its** tail.*
> *We have a boat; it is **our** boat; it is **ours**.*
> *They have a cat; it is **their** cat; it is **theirs**.*

- the interrogative and relative pronoun *who,* which changes to *whose*:

> ***Who** owns this car?* → ***Whose** is this car?*
> *the child **who** had a bike with a flat tyre* → *the child **whose** bike had a flat tyre*

You will find more information about the genitive case in the section 'Case of nouns' on page 66.

The subjective case and the objective case

The pronouns that have different forms for the subjective case (as the subject of a verb) and the objective case (as the object of a verb or after a preposition) are:

- most of the personal pronouns:

I (subjective); *me* (objective)   *we* (subjective); *us* (objective)
he (subjective); *him* (objective)   *they* (subjective); *them* (objective)
she (subjective); *her* (objective)

I/he/she/we/they can't swim. (subject of verb)
The receptionist ignored *me/him/her/us/them*. (direct object of verb)
Tell *me/him/her/us/them* what to do. (indirect object of verb)
The child smiled at *me/him/her/us/them*. (after preposition)

(Note that *you* and *it* do not have different subjective and objective forms. However, the subjective pronoun *thou*, meaning 'you (singular)', which is still used in some dialects of modern English, changes to *thee* in the objective case.)

- the interrogative and relative pronouns *who* (subjective) and *whom* (objective):

Who knows? / the people **who** live here (subject of verb)
Whom did you see? / the man **whom** she married (object of verb)
From **whom** is that letter? / John Smith, for **whom** she voted (after preposition)

In informal English, *who* is often used instead of *whom*, especially as the object of a verb:

Who did you see?   the man **who** she married

but you should still use *whom* directly after a preposition:

From whom is that letter? (not ***From who** is that letter?)
John Smith, **for whom** she voted (not *John Smith, **for who** she voted)

However, you could rephrase these examples in informal English as follows:

Who is that letter **from**?   John Smith, **who** she voted **for**

{CONTD}

'Jane and I' or 'Jane and me'?

Remember that the rules about case still apply when the pronoun is linked to a noun with *and*, *or*, etc.:

My friend and I *went to the theatre.* (not ***My friend and me** *went to the theatre.*)

We met *him and his wife* *on holiday.* (not **We met* *he and his wife* *on holiday.*)

Can you give *her and David* *a lift to the station?* (not **Can you give* *she and David* *a lift to the station?*)

This birthday card is from *Jane and me*. (not **This birthday card is from* *Jane and I*.)

If you are ever in doubt about which pronoun to use in a noun phrase containing *and*, *or*, etc., try removing the rest of the phrase:

[My friend and] *I* *went to the theatre.* (not **Me* *went to the theatre.*)

We met *him* *[and his wife]* *on holiday.* (not **We met* *he on holiday.*)

Can you give *her* *[and David]* *a lift to the station?* (not **Can you give* *she a lift to the station?*)

This birthday card is from *[Jane and]* *me*. (not **This birthday card is from* *I*.)

'She's younger than him' or 'she's younger than he'?

Which case should you use when the pronoun follows *than*?

The other team played better than *us*. or *The other team played better than* *we*.

His sister is younger than *him*. or *His sister is younger than* *he*.

The objective form is the more likely choice:

The other team played better than *us*. *His sister is younger than* *him*.

However, both these examples have a 'missing' verb at the end, and the pronoun is the subject of this verb. If you put the verb in, you must use the subjective form of the pronoun:

The other team played better than *His sister is younger than* *he is*.
we did.

But when the pronoun is the object of a 'missing' verb, it must remain in the objective case:

Anna likes Paul less than (she likes) *me*.
They gave her more than (they gave) *him*.

If you replace the objective pronouns *me* and *him* in these examples with the subjective pronouns *I* and *he*, the meaning changes:

*Anna likes Paul less than **I** (like Paul).*
*They gave her more than **he** (gave her).*

'It's I' or 'It's me'?

Should you use the subjective or objective form of a pronoun after *it is*, *these are*, etc.? In other words, which case should you use for the complement of the verb *be*?

• in formal English, the subjective form (*I, he, she, we, they*) is preferred:

*It was **I**.*   *These are **they**.*

(This 'rule' is based on Latin grammar.)

• in informal speech and writing the objective form (*me, him, her, us, them*) is more frequent:

*It was **me**.*   *These are them.*

IT WAS I

Sir Humphrey Appleby, the punctilious civil servant in *Yes Minister*, would not dream of saying 'It was me' instead of 'It was I':

'. . . in fact, not to put too fine a point on it, the individual in question was, it may surprise you to learn, the one whom your present interlocutor is in the habit of identifying by means of the perpendicular pronoun. . . . It was I,' he said. (Jonathan Lynn & Antony Jay, *The Complete Yes Minister*, BBC Worldwide, 'The Skeleton in the Cupboard')

Others are less careful:

Heedless of grammar, they all cried, 'That's him!' (Revd R. H. Barham, *The Jackdaw of Rheims*)

And some try so hard to get it right that they actually get it wrong:

'Whom are you?' he said, for he had been to night school. (George Ade, *Bang! Bang!: The Steel Box*)

Verbs

What is a verb?

A **verb** is a word that expresses action, change, being, having, etc.:

run, eat, operate, think, solidify, be, remain, have, resemble

You may have seen or heard a verb defined as a 'doing' word, especially in traditional grammar. This is a rather inadequate definition, as it implies only action, not being or having. If I *am* tired or I *have* a headache, for example, I am not 'doing' anything.

The verb is one of the main parts of a clause or sentence:

*They **arrived** at seven o'clock.*　*He **is** younger than you.*
***Come** here!*　***Are** these pictures for sale?*
*The lake **froze** last winter.*　*I **closed** the door and **locked** it.*
*She **has** a red car.*　*We **left** before the display **began**.*

It may consist of more than one word:

*She **was wearing** a red jacket.*　*This **may be** my only opportunity.*
Have** you **heard** the news?*　*We **should have been wearing
***Will** they **understand**?*　*lifejackets.*

The verb phrase

The verb element of a clause or sentence is called a **verb phrase**, whether it consists of a single word or more than one word:

*They **walked** across the field.*　*They **could have walked** across*
*They **were walking** across the field.*　*the field.*

Main verbs and auxiliary verbs

The **main verb** of a verb phrase is the word that expresses the meaning. All verb phrases contain a main verb. In the following sentences the main verb is *opened*:

*I **opened** the door.*　*Have you **opened** the door?*
*I had **opened** the door.*　*You should have **opened** the door.*

The main verb often has one or more other verbs in front of it, such as *had, is, will, should, can, might*, etc. These are called **auxiliary verbs**. In the following sentences the auxiliary verbs are in bold type:

*They **were** watching us.*　*They **may have been** watching us.*
*We **were being** watched.*　*We **may have been being***
watched.

You cannot use a main verb on its own in questions, or in negative sentences with *not* or *-n't*. In such cases you must add the auxiliary verb *do*:

They **missed** the train.

Did they **miss** the train? (not
  ***Missed** they the train?)

They **did not miss** the train. (not
  *They **missed not** the train.)

They **like** dogs.

Do they **like** dogs? (not ***Like**
  they dogs?)

They **don't like** dogs. (not *They
  liken't dogs.)

If the verb phrase already contains an auxiliary verb and a main verb, you move the auxiliary verb in front of the subject to form a question:

She **was carrying** a briefcase. → **Was** she **carrying** a briefcase?

If there is more than one auxiliary verb, you move the first one:

We **were being watched**. → **Were** we **being watched**?
They **could have been delayed**. → **Could** they **have been delayed**?

Similarly, to make the sentence negative you add *not* or *-n't* to the (first) auxiliary verb:

She **was carrying** a briefcase. → She **was not carrying** a briefcase.
They **could have been** delayed. → They **couldn't have been** delayed.

You will find more information about auxiliary verbs on pages 146–9.

Regular verbs and irregular verbs

There are two types of verb, regular verbs and irregular verbs. These terms relate to the way the verb changes its form in different tenses.

Regular verbs change their form according to a fixed pattern:

I **walk**; I **walked**; I **have walked**
it **exists**; it **existed**; it **has existed**

Irregular verbs do not follow this pattern:

I **eat**; I **ate** (not *I **eated**); I **have eaten** (not *I **have eated**)
it **blows**; it **blew** (not *it **blowed**); it **has blown** (not *it **has blowed**)

The majority of verbs are regular:

look, wash, arrive, travel, govern, remember, establish, etc.

However, many of the verbs you use most often are irregular:

be, have, go, do, take, put, come, see, cut, run, drive, sit, etc.

The forms of the verb

Unlike verbs in many foreign languages, most English verbs have only four or five forms. Each of these forms has a number of different uses.

Most regular verbs have four forms:

- the base form: *look, try, refer, organize*
- the *-s* form: *looks, tries, refers, organizes*
- the *-ing* form: *looking, trying, referring, organizing*
- the *-ed* form: *looked, tried, referred, organized*

Many irregular verbs have five forms:

- the base form: *go, swim, break, forget*
- the *-s* form: *goes, swims, breaks, forgets*
- the *-ing* form: *going, swimming, breaking, forgetting*
- an irregular equivalent of the *-ed* form used in the past tense: *went, swam, broke, forgot*
- an irregular equivalent of the *-ed* form used as the past participle: *gone, swum, broken, forgotten*

The base form

The **base form** has no added endings. It has three main uses:

- as the infinitive (often with *to*): *(to) be, (to) look, (to) mix, (to) come*

- in commands, instructions, requests, etc.:

  Be quiet!   **Mix** the flour and sugar together.
  Look at this strange insect!   **Come** in and close the door,
         please.

- in the present tense (for all persons except the third person singular): *I look, you come, we eat, they walk,* etc.

The -s form

The *-s* **form** is used in the third person singular (with *he, she, it,* etc.) of the present tense:

  he **listens**   Mary **works**
  the window **rattles**   summer **comes**

The -s form of regular verbs

For most regular verbs the -s form consists of the base form plus the ending -s: *listen/listens, work/works, rattle/rattles*

There are some exceptions:

- if the base form ends in -ch, -sh, -ss, -zz, or -x, you add -es: *reach/reaches, wash/washes, miss/misses, fizz/fizzes, mix/mixes,* etc. (Note also *quiz* → *quizzes, focus* → *focuses* or *focusses,* etc.)

- if the base form ends in -y, and there is at least one consonant before the -y, you change the -y to -ies: *try/tries, mystify/mystifies,* etc.

- base forms ending in -o may add -s or -es: *radio/radios, echo/echoes,* etc.

The -s form of irregular verbs

Most irregular verbs have 'regular' -s forms:

come/comes, sing/sings, break/breaks, see/sees, go/goes

There are three exceptions:

- the verb *be*, which is completely irregular in the present tense: *I am, you/we/they are, he/she/it is.*

- the verb *have*: *he/she/it has* (not **haves*).

- the verb *do*, which changes its pronunciation in the -s form: *he/she/it does* (rhyming with *buzz*, not with *booze*).

WHO FOOTS THE BILL?

When the same word can be used as a verb or noun, the -s form of the verb is usually the same as the plural form of the noun:

she cooks / four cooks	*it flies / many flies*
he rows / several rows	*it echoes / two echoes*

However, there are a number of exceptions:

I have sore **feet**.	*He* **foots** *the bill.*
The **geese** *are in the yard.*	*She* **gooses** *all the good-looking men.*
There are three **men** *outside.*	*Who* **mans** *the switchboard?*
It was crawling with **lice**.	*The weather* **louses** *up all our plans.*
The shop sells **knives**.	*He* **knifes** *his attacker.*
We baked four **loaves**.	*She* **loafs** *around all day.*

{CONTD}

The -*ing* form

For most regular and irregular verbs the -*ing* form consists of the base form plus the ending -*ing*:

> listen/listen**ing**, play/play**ing**, be/be**ing**, see/see**ing**

There are some exceptions:

> com**e**/com**ing**, involv**e**/involv**ing**, etc. (Note that the -e is not dropped in verbs such as singe/singe**ing**, to avoid confusion with sing/sing**ing**.)
> di**e**/d**ying**, ti**e**/t**ying**, vi**e**/v**ying**, etc.
> panic/panic**king**, picnic/picnic**king**, tarmac/tarmac**king**, etc.
> travel/travel**ling**, libel/libel**ling**, etc. (Note that in American English you do not double the -l: travel**ing**, libel**ing**.)
> bias → bia**sing** or bia**ssing**, focus → focu**sing** or focu**ssing**, etc.
> pad/pad**ding**, run/run**ning**, occur/occur**ring**, forget/forget**ting**, etc. (Note that if the main stress falls on an earlier syllable, you do not double the consonant: offer/offer**ing**, visit/visit**ing**, etc.)

Uses of the -*ing* form

The -*ing* form has three main uses:

- as the present participle of the verb

> I am **listening**, they were **going**, it might be **raining**

(You will find more information about the present participle on page 145.)

- as an adjective

an **amazing** achievement	**worrying** news
the **approaching** storm	**falling** rocks
a **nauseating** smell	**driving** rain

- as a noun, or in a phrase used like a noun:

Smoking is forbidden.	**Skiing** is not as easy as it looks.
Travelling by road is statistically more dangerous than flying.	He objects to **wearing a safety helmet**.

When an -*ing* form is used as a noun in this way it is sometimes called a **gerund**. This is a rather old-fashioned term.

A problem of usage may arise when an -*ing* form follows a noun or pronoun. Which of the following are 'correct'?

*He objects to **my** using the telephone.* or *He objects to **me** using the
   telephone.*
*This resulted in **Mary's** being dismissed.* or *This resulted in **Mary** being
   dismissed.*

In formal English, the sentences with *my* and *Mary's* are preferable. The
words *using* and *being* are behaving more like nouns than like verbs, so
the possessive forms are more appropriate. (As a simple test, try replacing
the *-ing* form with a noun: *my use of the telephone; Mary's dismissal.*)

In informal English, you are more likely to hear or say *me* and *Mary.*
The following sentence from Jane Austen's *Sense and Sensibility* would
sound very stilted in modern speech:

Elinor was prevented from making any reply . . . by the door's being
thrown open, the servant's announcing Mr Ferrars, and Edward's
immediately walking in.

However, if the phrase containing the *-ing* form comes at the beginning
of the sentence, the possessive may be preferable even in informal English:

My *using the telephone seems to annoy him.* (not ***Me** *using the
   telephone seems to annoy him.*)

The *-ed* form

The *-ed* **form** (or its irregular equivalent) is used in the past tense and as
the past participle:

*They **accepted** our offer.*	*Our offer has been **accepted**.*
*They have **accepted** our offer.*	*Having **accepted** our offer, . . .*

It may also be used as an adjective:

an **astonished** look	**faded** curtains
broken glass	**frozen** food

The -ed form of regular verbs

For most regular verbs the *-ed* form consists of the base form plus the
ending *-ed* (or *-d,* if the base form ends in *-e*):

*listen/listen**ed**, work/work**ed**, accept/accept**ed**, race/race**d**, tie/tie**d***

There are some exceptions:

*try/tr**ied**, panic/panic**ked**, travel/travel**led**, bias → bias**ed** or bias**sed**,
pad/pad**ded**, occur/occur**red**, etc.*

{CONTD}

The -*ed* form of irregular verbs

Most irregular verbs do not have an -*ed* form. They form the past tense and past participle in a variety of different ways.

- Some use the base form unchanged for the past tense and past participle:

  Cut *the string with a sharp knife.* (base form)
  *I **cut** my leg yesterday.* (past tense)
  *You have **cut** the bread too thinly.* (past participle)

Other verbs of this type include *burst, cost, hit, hurt, let, put, shut, split,* etc.
  The verbs *come* and *run* use the base form for the past participle, but have an irregular past tense:

  come; *I **came**; I have **come*****   ***run***; *I **ran**; I have **run***

- Many have different forms for the past tense and past participle:

  do; *I **did**; I have **done***   ***go***; *I **went**; I have **gone***
  draw; *I **drew**; I have **drawn***   ***lie***; *I **lay**; I have **lain***
  fly; *I **flew**; I have **flown***   ***see***; *I **saw**; I have **seen***

The past participle of this type of verb often ends in -*en*: *eat/ate/eaten, fall/fell/fallen, give/gave/given,* etc.

In most of these verbs the vowel sound of the base form changes in the past tense and past participle. These changes sometimes form a pattern that is followed in other verbs:

  freeze/froze/frozen, speak/spoke/spoken, weave/wove/woven, etc.
  drive/drove/driven, ride/rode/ridden, write/wrote/written, etc.
  blow/blew/blown, grow/grew/grown, know/knew/known, etc.
  begin/began/begun, drink/drank/drunk, ring/rang/rung,
  swim/swam/swum, etc.

- Others use the same irregular form for the past tense and past participle:

  have; *I **had**; I have **had***   *hold*; *I **held**, I have **held***
  hear; *I **heard**; I have **heard***   *stand*; *I **stood**; I have **stood***

The past participle of this type of verb often ends in -*t*:

  build/built, buy/bought, catch/caught, fight/fought, lose/lost, meet/met,
  seek/sought, shoot/shot, sit/sat, teach/taught, think/thought.

Once again, some verbs change in the same way as others:

  bind/bound, find/found, grind/ground, wind/wound, etc.
  creep/crept, keep/kept, sleep/slept, sweep/swept, weep/wept, etc.

bend/bent, lend/lent, send/sent, spend/spent, etc.
cling/clung, fling/flung, sting/stung, swing/swung, wring/wrung, etc.

- A number of verbs have two possible forms for the past tense and past participle, a regular *-ed* form and an irregular form ending in *-t*:

burn → *burn**ed*** or *burn**t***	*smell* → *smell**ed*** or *smel**t***
kneel → *kneel**ed*** or *knel**t***	*spell* → *spell**ed*** or *spel**t***
leap → *leap**ed*** or *leap**t***	*spill* → *spill**ed*** or *spil**t***
learn → *learn**ed*** or *learn**t***	*spoil* → *spoil**ed*** or *spoil**t***

- Some have a regular *-ed* form in the past tense and two possible forms for the past participle, one regular and the other irregular:

__Mow__ the lawn. (base form)
*I **mowed** the lawn yesterday.* (past tense)
*Have you **mowed** [or **mown**] the lawn yet?* (past participle)

Other verbs of this type include *hew, saw, sew, show,* and *sow.*

- Finally, there are a few verbs that have a regular *-ed* form with one meaning and an irregular form with another meaning. (The meaning of the irregular verb is usually the more common of the two.) Here are some examples with the verbs *hang, shine,* and *weave*:

*The assassins were **hanged**.*	*The pictures were **hung** on hooks.*
*I **shined** my shoes.*	*I **shone** my torch into the cave.*
*She **weaved** her way through the traffic.*	*They **wove** the thread into cloth.*

WHO'D HAVE THUNK IT?

Some irregular past participles have fallen into disuse, surviving only as adjectives or in fixed phrases:

wrought *iron* (old past participle of *work*)
writ *large* (old past participle of *write*)

A few survive in American or dialect use. For example, the Americans use *gotten* as the past participle of *get,* but in British English this form is found only in phrases like *ill-gotten gains,* or in compounds such as *forgotten* and *begotten.*

At the same time, 'new' irregular past forms are sometimes coined for fun. You may have heard *brung* (for *brought*) and *thunk* (for *thought*), and these terms have found their way into some dictionaries of slang.

Finite verbs and non-finite verbs

The forms of a verb can be divided into two groups, finite and non-finite.

Finite verbs

The **finite** forms of a verb include

- the base form when it is used in the present tense or in commands, instructions etc.:

    They **belong** to the same club.   **Open** the window.

- the -*s* form:

    It always **rains** at the weekend.   He **has** no brothers or sisters.
    The train never **comes** on time.   She **is** fond of animals.

- the -*ed* form (or irregular equivalent) when it is used in the past tense:

    They **belonged** to the same club.   He **had** no brothers or sisters.
    We **walked** home.   She **was** fond of animals.

Non-finite verbs

The **non-finite** forms of a verb include

- the base form when it is used in the infinitive: *to belong, to open.*
- the -*ing* form when it is used as the present participle: *belonging, opening.*
- the -*ed* form (or irregular equivalent) when it is used as the past participle: *opened, invited, worn, sold.*

Finite verb phrases and non-finite verb phrases

A **finite verb phrase** contains a verb in finite form:

    I **live** in Kent.   He **left** on Friday.

A finite verb phrase may also consist of a finite form followed by a non-finite form:

    He **had left** three days earlier. (*had* is finite, *left* is non-finite)

It may contain more than one non-finite form:

    I **have been living** in Kent for two years. (*have* is finite, *been* and *living* are non-finite)

A **non-finite verb phrase** consists of one or more non-finite verb forms. It does not contain a verb in finite form:

> *Living* in Kent, . . .   *Having been invited* to
> *Encouraged* by our success, . . .   wedding, . . .

Finite clauses and non-finite clauses

A **finite clause** is a clause that contains a finite verb phrase. It may be a complete sentence, or part of a sentence:

> *He drives a red car.*   *If you had brought an umbrella, . . .*

A **non-finite clause** is a clause that contains a non-finite verb phrase:

> *To solve this problem . . .*   *. . . while cooking the dinner.*

The infinitive

The **infinitive** is the base form of the verb, often preceded by *to*. It has a wide range of uses, some of which are listed below.

Uses of the infinitive with *to*

- after a verb: *He forgot **to close** the window.*
- after an adjective: *It is hard **to understand**.*
- after a noun or pronoun: *We have plenty of work **to do**.*
- as part of an adverbial phrase: ***To be honest**, I don't care.*

TO BE OR NOT TO BE

The infinitive with *to* is sometimes used as the subject of a verb. This is rare in everyday speech and writing, but examples can be found in literature:

To err is human, to forgive, divine. (Alexander Pope, *An Essay on Criticism*)

To travel hopefully is a better thing than to arrive. (Robert Louis Stevenson, *Virginibus Puerisque*)

To lose one parent . . . may be regarded as a misfortune; to lose both looks like carelessness. (Oscar Wilde, *The Importance of Being Earnest*)

{CONTD}

Uses of the infinitive without *to*

- after the auxiliary verbs *can, will, should, may, must*, etc.:

  I can't **find** my diary.   They may **know** the answer.
  It will **take** too long.   He must **be** her brother.
  Should I **shut** the door?

- after the auxiliary verb *do* used in questions and negatives:

  Do you **like** smoked salmon?   We didn't **stay** long.

- after verbs such as *see, hear, feel*, etc.:

  I saw him **fall**.   She heard them **leave**.

- after the verbs *make* and *let*:

  Make him **apologize**.   We let her **stay**.

- after *rather*:

  I'd rather **watch** television.

More complex infinitives

You can use the auxiliary verbs *have* and *be* to form more complex infinitives. These include

- the perfect infinitive, made up of *to have* + past participle:

  He expects us **to have read** his   I'm glad **to have known** her.
  novel.

- the passive infinitive, made up of *to be* + past participle:

  It was annoying **to be treated** so   They don't want **to be pitied**.
  badly.

- the progressive infinitive, made up of *to be* + present participle:

  She is believed **to be using** a false   He hopes **to be playing** football
  name.   again soon.

- others made up of *to have been* + past or present participle:

  It would have been nice **to have**   They appear **to have been**
  been asked.   **cheating**.

The participles

There are two participles, the present participle and the past participle.

The present participle

The **present participle** is the *-ing* form of the verb. It is used with the auxiliary verb *be* to form finite verb phrases relating to present time, future time or past time:

> He **is wearing** a blue jumper.
> I **am going** to London tomorrow.
> We **may be moving** house next month.
>
> She **was eating** an apple.
> You **should have been listening**.
> I **had been neglecting** my studies.

You can also use the present participle in non-finite clauses:

> I changed my mind after **reading** the article in the local paper.
> Before **replacing** the bulb, disconnect the power supply.

You will find more information about the *-ing* form, including its use as a noun or adjective, on page 138.

The past participle

The **past participle** is the *-ed* form (or irregular equivalent) of the verb. It is used with the auxiliary verb *have* to form finite verb phrases relating to past time:

> She **has broken** her promise.
> The dog **had followed** me home.
>
> This **would have ruined** our plans.

You can also use the past participle

- with the auxiliary verb *be* to form passive verb phrases relating to past, present, or future time:

> The letter **was delivered** to the wrong address.
> Her purse **had been stolen**.
>
> The rooms **are cleaned** every day.
> They **will be expected** to pay for their meals.

- in non-finite clauses: **Helped** by my friends, I overcame the problem.

- as an adjective: **faded** curtains; **broken** glass

You will find more information about the *-ed* form and its irregular equivalents on pages 139–41.

Auxiliary verbs

An **auxiliary verb** is a word like *is, have, do, will, should, could, may*, etc., that comes in front of a main verb:

> They **were** watching us.
> He **had** opened the door.
> **Can** she swim?

> It **might** rain.
> **Do** you think I **should** accept their offer?

In verb phrases it is usually the auxiliary verb that changes for person, number, tense, etc.

> The child **is** watching us.
> The children **are** watching us.
> The children **were** watching us.

> I **have** opened the door.
> Somebody **has** opened the door.
> Somebody **had** opened the door.

There is often more than one auxiliary verb in a verb phrase:

> We **were being** watched.
> They **may have been** watching us.

> We **may have been being** watched.

There are two types of auxiliary verb: primary verbs and modal verbs.

Primary verbs

A **primary verb** is a verb that you can use as a main verb or as an auxiliary verb. There are three primary verbs – *be, have,* and *do*. Here are some examples of their use.

- as a main verb:

> My cousin **is** a teacher.
> Mike **was** angry.

> They **have** four children.
> She **did** nothing to help.

- as an auxiliary verb:

> My cousin **is coming** to stay.
> Mike **was losing** his temper.

> They **have moved** house.
> She **did** not **know** what to say.

- as auxiliary verb and main verb in the same verb phrase:

> Jack **was being** very secretive.
> **Did** I **do** the right thing?

> My grandmother **has had** a heart attack.

Unlike modal verbs, primary verbs change their form in the present tense (*am/are/is, have/has, do/does*). They also have *-ing* forms (*being, having, doing*) and past forms (*was/were, had, did*):

You use *be* as an auxiliary verb

- before a present participle, to show that an action or state is progressive or continuous:

    *I **am reading** the paper.*   *I **have been living** here since 1984.*
    *I **was wearing** a long skirt.*   *I **had been waiting** for an hour.*

- before a past participle, to form a passive verb phrase:

    *The seeds **are crushed** to extract the oil.*   *The stolen car **has been found**.*
        *The price **had been reduced**.*

You use *have* as an auxiliary verb

- before a past participle, to express past time:

    *I **have lost** my key.*   *I **had forgotten** their address.*

You use *do* as an auxiliary verb

- when you want to ask a question, or change a statement into a question:

    *Cats **chase** mice.* → ***Do** cats **chase** mice?*

- when you want to make a sentence negative by adding *not* or *-n't*:

    *Mice **chase** cats.* → *Mice **do not chase** cats.*

DO YOU HAVE A PROBLEM?

There are two ways of making a statement or asking a question when the main verb is *have*. In British English, especially informal conversation, you would probably use *have got*:

*I**'ve got** a headache.*   ***Have** you **got** enough money?*

In American English, or in formal British English, you might say:

*I **have** a headache.*   ***Do** you **have** enough money?*

In answer to the question 'Have you got enough money?' or 'Do you have enough money?', a British person will say 'No, I haven't', whereas an American will say 'No, I don't'. The same applies to the tags *haven't you* and *don't you*:

*You've got a problem, **haven't you**?* (British)
*You have a problem, **don't you**?* (American)

{CONTD}

Modal verbs

A **modal verb** can only be used as an auxiliary verb. The modal verbs include *will*, *would*, *shall*, *should*, *can*, *could*, *may*, *might*, and *must*. The verb that comes after a modal verb is in the base form (without endings):

*It **will cost** too much.*   ***May** I **borrow** your car?*

Unlike primary verbs, modal verbs do not change their form in the present tense and do not have *-ing* forms:

*I **might** fall.*	*We **might** fall.*
*You **might** fall.*	*They **might** fall.*
*He/She/It **might** fall.*	

Modal verbs are sometimes followed by the primary verbs *be* or *have*:

*She **should be** working faster.*   *You **could have** waited.*
*The bottles **can be** recycled.*   *He **must have been** offered the job.*

The meanings of modal verbs

Modal verbs may express:

- possibility, probability, or certainty:

  *It **may** rain.*   *The letter **should** arrive tomorrow.*
  *She **might** have forgotten.*   *This **must** be the way out.*
  *He **could** be hiding.*   *You **will** fail.*

- ability:

  ***Can** you swim?*   *He **couldn't** read her handwriting.*

- requests or suggestions:

  ***May** we have a look?*   ***Shall** I open a window?*
  ***Would** you move your car, please.*   *You **could** try a different shampoo.*

- offers or invitations:

  ***Can** I help?*   ***Will** you stay for dinner?*
  ***Would** you like to come with us?*

- permission:

  *You **may** have one more.*   ***Can** I go now?*

- obligation:

  She **shall** pay for the damage.   He **must** apologize.

Note that when you change a sentence from present time to past time, you sometimes have to replace *will*, *can*, or *may* with *would*, *could*, or *might*:

  I think it **will** rain. → I thought it **would** rain.
  He knows you **can** see him. → He knew you **could** see him.
  She says we **may** stay. → She said we **might** stay.

Remember, however, that the use of *would*, *could*, and *might* is not restricted to past time.

Verbs resembling auxiliary verbs

There are a number of other verbs and verb phrases that behave like modal auxiliary verbs. These include *need (to)*, *ought (to)*, *dare*, *used to*, *be able to*, *be about to*, *be going to*, *have to*, *had better*, *would rather*, etc. They always come before the base form of a verb, sometimes with *to*:

  You **need to see** a doctor.   **Were** they **able to help**?
  She **needn't tell** him.   The water **is about to boil**.
  Need I **wait**?   It **is going to rain**.
  You **ought to see** a doctor.   You **have to turn** the handle.
  She **daren't tell** him.   She **had better try** again.
  I **used to work** in a bank.   He **would rather go** to Spain.

(The verbs *need*, *ought (to)*, *dare*, and *used to* are sometimes called **marginal modals** or **semi-modals**. Verbs beginning with *be* or *have*, such as *be about to* or *have to*, are sometimes called **semi-auxiliaries** or **phrasal auxiliaries**.)

The verbs *need* and *dare* have an *-s* form:

  He **needs** to find a job.   If she **dares** to refuse, . . .

The verbs *need*, *be able to*, *be about to*, *be going to*, and *have to* may have another auxiliary in front of them:

  She **will need** to apply for a visa.   The water **must be about to** boil.
  You **should be able to** see it from   It **may be going to** rain.
    there.   He **might have to** sell his boat.

Other types of verb

Catenative verbs

A **catenative verb** is a type of verb that you can put in front of other verbs. Catenative verbs include *appear, begin, come, expect, fail, get, go, happen, help, manage, seem, stop, want*. They usually come before a verb in the base form, linked by *to*:

She **appears to like** you.

It **began to rain**.

He **came to see** us yesterday.

They **expect to win** this match.

I **fail to understand** why.

She **went to open** the door.

Do you **happen to know** their address?

We eventually **managed to find** them.

He **seems to have** a problem.

I **want to go** home.

The name **catenative** comes from the Latin word for 'chain'. It is applied to these verbs because they link to other verbs like a chain. Some catenatives also link to each other:

How did he **manage to fail** to notice all the warning signs?

She **seemed to want to help** to solve the crime.

You can use the present participle of a verb after a few catenative verbs:

The orchestra **began playing**.

We **went sailing** on Saturday.

The child **stopped crying**.

And you can use the past participle after *get*:

I **got promoted** last month.

He **got involved** in an argument.

The verb *help* can be followed by the infinitive of a verb, with or without *to*:

The drugs will **help (to) ease** the pain.

But you use the present participle after *can't help, couldn't help*, etc.:

I **can't help being** clumsy.

We **couldn't help laughing**.

A catenative verb sometimes has a direct object:

She **expected the car** to start immediately.

I **got my hair** cut.

Counselling **helped me** (to) cope.

He **wants you** to stay.

We **watched them** play.

Copular verbs

A **copular verb**, also called a **linking verb**, is a verb like *be, become, remain, seem, appear, grow, turn, feel, sound, smell, taste,* etc. A copular verb usually links its subject to a complement (a word or phrase that provides further information about the subject):

*The water **is** hot.*
*My daughter **is** a solicitor.*
*The wind **became** stronger.*
*He **remained** our friend.*

*Jenny **seems** pleased.*

*The days **grew** longer.*
*His hair **turned** grey.*
*I **feel** a fool.*
*Your plans **sound** rather ambitious.*
*The orange **tasted** bitter.*

You will find more information about copular verbs in the section 'The complement' on pages 33–4.

WE PRIDE OURSELVES ON OUR OBJECTIVITY

The verb *pride oneself* is a **reflexive verb**. In other words, its direct object is a reflexive pronoun (i.e. one ending in *-self* or *-selves* that refers back to the subject). There is a small group of English verbs that can only be used reflexively:

absent oneself, demean oneself, perjure oneself, pride oneself

You can absent yourself or perjure yourself, but you cannot absent or perjure anybody else.

A number of verbs have a reflexive meaning in which the reflexive pronoun is optional and often omitted:

*I **washed** (**myself**) in the stream.*
*The children rarely **dress** (**themselves**) before breakfast.*

You usually add the pronoun if you want to draw attention to the reflexive nature of the action:

*I washed my clothes and then I **washed myself**.*
*Children should be able to **dress themselves** by this age.*

With other verbs the reflexive pronoun is compulsory:

*She **taught herself** to play the trumpet.*
*He **hated himself** for what he had done.*

{CONTD}

Multi-word verbs

A **multi-word verb** is a verb followed by an adverb, a preposition, or both. The adverb or preposition is called a **particle**. Here are some examples:

let down (verb + adverb): *She apologized for **letting** him **down**.*
look after (verb + preposition): *I **look after** my neighbour's children during the holidays.*
make up for (verb + adverb + preposition): *This year's profit should **make up for** last year's loss.*

A multi-word verb is a complete unit of meaning. In the above examples *let down* means 'disappoint', *look after* means 'take care of', and *make up for* means 'compensate for'.

Sometimes the same combination of words may be a multi-word verb in one context but not in another. Compare the following examples:

*They are **looking into** the matter.*   *They are **looking into** the cage.*

The first sentence contains the multi-word verb *look into*, meaning 'investigate'. The second sentence contains the verb *look* and the preposition *into* used independently. You could substitute other words for *look* and *into* without making nonsense of the second sentence:

*They are **staring into** the cage.*   *They are **looking out of** the cage.*

You cannot do this with the first sentence:

They are **staring into the matter.*   **They are **looking out of** the matter.*

Here are some more pairs of examples:

*We **ran out of** petrol.* (multi-word verb) / *We **ran out of** the house.*
*He **stood by** his promise.* (multi-word verb) / *He **stood by** the gate.*

You can say *we ran into the house* or *he sat by the gate*, but you cannot say **we ran into petrol* or **he sat by his promise*.

Types of multi-word verb

Multi-word verbs come in three flavours: phrasal verbs, prepositional verbs, and phrasal-prepositional verbs.

A **phrasal verb** has an adverb as its particle: *bring up, call off, carry on, knock out*, etc.

A **prepositional verb** has a preposition as its particle: *care for, come across* (meaning 'find'), *run into, take after*, etc.

A **phrasal-prepositional verb** has two particles, an adverb and a preposition: *get away with, go in for, look forward to, put up with*, etc.

(You will sometimes find the term **phrasal verb** used to cover all three types of multi-word verb.)

Many of the adverb particles of phrasal verbs are words that can also be prepositions, e.g. *up, off, on*. (Similarly, some of the particles of prepositional verbs can also be adverbs, e.g. *across, after*.) So you may find it hard to tell the difference between a phrasal verb and a prepositional verb, especially when the particle is followed by a noun phrase:

    to **bring up** a subject   to **come across** a rare book
    to **call off** a strike   to **take after** one's father

In cases like this, try moving the particle to follow the noun phrase. If it can be moved, you have a phrasal verb. If it cannot be moved, you have a prepositional verb:

    to **bring up** a subject (phrasal verb) / to **bring** a subject **up**
    to **call off** a strike (phrasal verb) / to **call** a strike **off**

    to **come across** a rare book (prepositional verb) / not *to **come** a rare book **across**
    to **take after** one's father (prepositional verb) / not *to **take** one's father **after**

Alternatively, you can try replacing the noun phrase with a pronoun such as *him, her, it*, or *them*. The pronoun has to go before the particle in a phrasal verb and after the particle in a prepositional verb:

    They've **called it off**. (phrasal verb) / not *They've **called off it**.
    She **takes after him**. (prepositional verb) / not *She **takes him after**.

Transitive verbs and intransitive verbs

Depending on the way they are used in a particular sentence, verbs can be divided into two groups, transitive and intransitive.

Transitive verbs

A **transitive** verb has a direct object:

I **hate spiders**.   She **made a mistake**.

If you remove the direct object, the sentence is incomplete:

*I **hate**.   *She **made**.

Note that the object of a transitive verb does not have to be a noun phrase. It may be a clause, or a piece of direct speech. In the following examples the verbs in bold type are all transitive:

I **noticed** that the window was   They **explained** how it worked.
    broken.   'Where is it?' she **asked**.

Intransitive verbs

An **intransitive** verb does not have a direct object:

The moon **appeared**.   Prices **are rising**.

It may, however, be followed by a word or phrase used adverbially:

Leaves **fell from the trees**.   She **waited for several hours**.

Some intransitive verbs cannot be used without an adverbial in some senses:

A leather jacket **lay on the bed**. (not *A leather jacket **lay**.)
I **live near the river**. (not *I **live**.)

Verbs used transitively and intransitively

Some verbs (e.g. *bring, find, like, use*) are always transitive. Some verbs (e.g. *appear, die, happen, rise*) are always intransitive. However, there are many verbs that are transitive in some uses and intransitive in others:

He **was typing** a letter. (transitive)   Jane **won** the race. (transitive)
He **was typing**. (intransitive)   Jane **won**. (intransitive)

Sometimes the transitive meaning is quite different from the intransitive meaning:

> She **ran** the company for several years. (transitive)
> She **ran** to the station. (intransitive)

Sometimes you can make the direct object of a transitive verb into the subject of the same verb used intransitively:

> Her remarks **increased** our curiosity. (transitive)
> Our curiosity **increased**. (intransitive)
>
> Somebody **rang** the doorbell. (transitive)
> The doorbell **rang**. (intransitive)

Ditransitive verbs

A **ditransitive** verb has a direct object and an indirect object:

> I **gave** the child a present.   They **sent** me an application form.
> Neil **bought** Laura a cup of coffee.   He **threw** the dog a bone.

You will find more information about direct and indirect objects on page 32.

LET SLEEPING DOGS LIE

The verbs *lay* and *lie* cause problems of usage in some regions. In standard English, *lay* is usually transitive, and *lie* is always intransitive:

*Hens **lay** eggs.*   ***Lie** on the bed.*
***Lay** the blanket on the bed.*   *The town **lies** to the east of Paris.*

Confusion may arise because the past tense of lie is lay:

***Lay** the blanket on the bed. (present tense of lay)*
*The blanket **lay** on the bed. (past tense of lie)*

In standard English, the verb *lay* is only used *intransitively* in the sense of 'to lay eggs':

*The hens are **laying** well this week.*

Note also that the verb *lie* is usually followed by an adverbial, with one or two exceptions:

*The snow didn't **lie**.*   *Let sleeping dogs **lie**.*

Mood

The **mood** of a verb tells you about its general meaning or the way it is used in a particular sentence. There are three moods:

- the **indicative** mood, used for statements or questions of fact

  *I **have** no children.*　　　　　*She **will be** late.*
  *He **went** straight home.*　　　***Are** these your car keys?*

- the **subjunctive** mood, used to express a demand, a wish, a possibility, a supposition, etc.

  *We insist that he **leave** at once.*　*Far **be** it from me to stand in your*
  *If I **were** prime minister, . . .*　　*way.*

- the imperative mood, used in commands, instructions, requests, etc.

  ***Come** here!*　　　　　　　　　***Cook** the meringue in a cool oven.*

The indicative mood

The indicative is the most common of the three moods. Verbs in the indicative mood may change their form for person, number, tense, etc.: *They **work** in a bank. / He **works** in a bank. / She **worked** in a bank.*

The subjunctive mood

The subjunctive is the least common mood. It has three main uses.

- In formal English the subjunctive is used in *that*-clauses after verbs like *insist, demand, ask, request, propose, intend, suggest, recommend,* etc. This is called the **mandative subjunctive**. For the mandative subjunctive you use the base form of the verb. In other words, you do not add *-s* in the third person singular and you use *be* instead of *am, is,* or *are*.

  *I suggested that she **stay**.*　　　*She requested that the ring **be** sold.*
  *We insist that he **leave** at once.*　*I demand that the case **be***
  　　　　　　　　　　　　　　　　reopened.

You can also use the mandative subjunctive in *that*-clauses after nouns like *demand, request, proposal, suggestion,* etc., and after adjectives like *essential, vital, necessary, important,* etc.:

  *our demand that the road **be** closed to through traffic*
  *It is essential that the patient **sign** the consent form.*

• The subjunctive is also used in some fixed expressions. This is called the **formulaic subjunctive** or **optative subjunctive**. Like the mandative subjunctive, it consists of the base form of the verb:

God **save** the queen!   Woe **betide** anybody who makes
Heaven **forbid**!   a noise!

In the formulaic subjunctive the subject often comes after the verb:

So **be it**.   Long **live the king**!
Be that as it may, ...   **Perish the thought**!

• A third type of subjunctive is used in formal English to express a hypothetical condition. This is called the *were-*subjunctive, because it uses *were* in place of *was*. It is most often found in clauses beginning with *if, even if, as if, as though, suppose, supposing,* etc.

if I **were** prime minister.   even if she **were** to apologize.

It is also used after the verb *wish*:

I wish it **were** true.   She wished she **were** at home.

In informal English, you often use the indicative in place of the *were-*subjunctive:

I felt as if I **was** flying.   She wished she **was** at home.

The mandative subjunctive is also often replaced by the indicative, sometimes with *should*, especially in British English:

I suggested that she **should stay**.   We insist that he **leaves** at once.

The imperative mood

You use the imperative mood in commands, and often in instructions, requests, advice, etc. Like most forms of the subjunctive, it consists of the base form of the verb:

Come here!   **Take** a seat.
Cook the meringue in a cool oven.   **Try** again.

You make the imperative negative by putting *don't* or *do not* before the verb:

Don't be rude!   **Do not exceed** the stated dose.

You will find more information about the imperative mood in the section 'Directives' on page 40.

The active voice and the passive voice

You can often express the meaning of a sentence in two different ways:

Sue broke the cup.   *The cup was broken by Sue.*

The first sentence uses the **active voice**, the second uses the **passive voice**. Here are some more examples:

The cat is chasing the mouse. (active)
The mouse is being chased by the cat. (passive)

My uncle has bought the house. (active)
The house has been bought by my uncle. (passive)

Changing the active to the passive

From the three pairs of examples above, you will see that a number of changes take place when an active sentence becomes passive.

- the active verb phrases (*broke, is chasing, has bought*) change to passive verb phrases (*was broken, is being chased, has been bought*).

- the subject of the active verb phrase (*Sue, the cat, my uncle*) moves to follow the passive verb phrase. It becomes the **agent** of the passive sentence, with *by* in front of it.

- the object of the active verb phrase (*the cup, the mouse, the house*) moves in front of the passive verb phrase and becomes the subject.

Active verbs and passive verbs

An active verb phrase may consist of a single main verb. A passive verb phrase always contains some form of the auxiliary verb *be* followed by a past participle. Note how the verb phrase changes in the following examples:

*Sam **drives** the minibus.*   → *The minibus **is driven** by Sam.*
*Sam **drove** the minibus.*   → *The minibus **was driven** by Sam.*
*Sam **will drive** the minibus.*   → *The minibus **will be driven** by Sam.*

Only transitive verbs can be made passive. Intransitive verbs are always active. However, there are some transitive verbs that you cannot change from active to passive:

*The bird **resembles** a jay.* (not **A jay **is resembled** by the bird.*)
*The students **lacked** interest.* (not **Interest **was lacked** by the students.*)

You cannot make a reflexive verb (see page 151) passive:

*The dog **scratched itself**.* (not ******Itself was scratched** by the dog.*)

Similarly, some passive verbs cannot be made active:

*You **are supposed** to use a pen.* (not **They **suppose** you to use a pen.*)

Use of the passive

Most guides to style and usage tell you not to overuse the passive voice. However, it is sometimes impossible or undesirable to change a passive sentence to an active one, especially when the agent is not known:

Graffiti had been daubed all over the walls.
A number of ideas were put forward at the meeting.

You can make these sentences active by 'guessing' at the agent, but you have no way of knowing how many people were involved:

Somebody had daubed graffiti all over the walls.
A number of people put forward ideas at the meeting.

The passive agent

It is not always necessary to include the agent in a passive sentence:

*The fence had been blown down (**by the wind**).*
*The French fought the English and were defeated (**by the English**).*

GETTING STARTED

You sometimes use the verb *get* instead of the verb *be* in passive verb phrases, especially in informal English:

*The hero **is** killed at the end.* or *The hero **gets** killed at the end.*
*We may not **be** invited.* or *We may not **get** invited.*
***Were** all the cakes eaten?* or ***Did** all the cakes **get** eaten?*

But if the agent is mentioned, sometimes only *be* can be used:

*They **were** married by her uncle.* (not **They **got** married by her uncle.*)

When the past participle that follows *be* or *get* is behaving more like an adjective than a verb, *get* may have a meaning closer to 'become':

*We **were** lost.*	*If the tyres **are** damaged, ...*
*We **got** lost.*	*If the tyres **get** damaged, ...*

Tense

The **tense** of a verb tells you what time it refers to – past, present, or future:

*I **live** in Kent.* (present tense)   *I **lived** in Kent.* (past tense)

In English (unlike many other languages), the form of the main verb can only change from the present tense to the past tense, as in the examples above. All other 'tenses', including the future, contain an auxiliary verb. For this reason, some modern grammars say that English has only two tenses, the present tense and the past tense.

The present tense

The **simple present tense** usually consists of the base form of the verb, with the *-s* form in the third person singular:

I **run**	we **run**	I **have**	we **have**
you **run**	you **run**	you **have**	you **have**
he/she/it **runs**	they **run**	he/she/it **has**	they **have**

The verb *be* is the only exception:

*I **am**, you **are**, he/she/it **is**, we **are**, they **are***

Present time can also be expressed with the verb *be* and the present participle (*-ing* form):

I **am running**	we **are running**
you **are running**	you **are running**
he/she/it **is running**	they **are running**

You will find more information about this verb form in the section 'Aspect' on page 165.

Uses of the present tense

The present tense usually expresses present time.

- the **state present** describes a state or timeless condition:

  *Rome **is** the capital of Italy.*   *Water **boils** at 100°C.*

- the **habitual present** describes a habitual or recurring action or event:

  *I **play** badminton on Tuesdays.*   *It always **rains** at the weekend.*

- the **instantaneous present** describes an action or event as it happens:

  *Conroy **serves** to Latham, . . .* (sports commentary)
  *The butler **enters**, carrying a tray of glasses.* (stage direction)

The present tense can also refer to past time:

- with verbs like *say, tell, hear, understand,* etc.:

  *Jack **tells** me you've offered him a job.*
  *I **hear** they've sold their house.*

- in jokes and narratives:

  *A man **walks** into a bar and **says**, 'Ouch!' – it was an iron bar.*
  *. . . so I **run** into the house and **tell** my parents there's a snake on the patio, and of course they **don't believe** me . . .*

- in newspaper headlines, captions, etc.:

  *Prime minister **resigns**.* (headline)
  *The Prince of Wales **chats** to patients on his visit to the new children's hospital yesterday.* (caption)

The present tense can also refer to future time:

  *She **flies** to Paris this afternoon.*
  *If the two sides **reach** an agreement at tomorrow's meeting, . . .*

The past tense

The **simple past tense** consists of the *-ed* form (or irregular equivalent) of the verb:

  *I **followed**, you **followed**, he/she/it **followed**, we **followed**, they **followed***
  *I **ran**, you **ran**, he/she/it **ran**, we **ran**, they **ran***

The verb *be* is the only verb that does not use the same form for all persons of the past tense: *I **was**, you **were**, he/she/it **was**, we **were**, they **were***.

Past time can also be expressed in many other ways:

*I **have followed***	*I **have been following***
*I **had followed***	*I **had been following***
*I **was following***	*I **used to follow***

You will find more information about most of these verb forms in the section 'Aspect' on page 164.

{CONTD}

Uses of the past tense

The past tense usually expresses past time. It may refer to

- a state:

  *She **was** angry.*   *They **lived** in New York.*

- a habitual action or event:

  *He **visited** his mother once a month. We **travelled** to school by bus.*

Note that you can also express habitual action in the past with *used to* or *would*:

  *The dog **barked** at every car that went past.*
  *The dog **used to bark** at every car that went past.*
  *The dog **would bark** at every car that went past.*

- a single specific action or event:

  *I **opened** the door.*   *The company **went** out of business.*

The past tense can also refer to present time

- in indirect speech:

  *He **said** he **had** a headache.* (i.e. he said, 'I have a headache.')
  *They **told** us she **was** a spy.* (i.e. they said, 'She is a spy.')

- the **attitudinal past** is used in tentative or polite statements, questions, etc.:

  *I **wondered** if I should wait a bit longer.* (i.e. I am still wondering)
  *Is that all, or **did** you **want** something else?* (i.e. do you want . . . ?)

- the **hypothetical past** is used in clauses beginning with *if* or following the verb *wish*:

  *If I **had** a million pounds, . . .*   *I wish they **lived** a bit closer.*

Future time

Future time can be expressed in various ways:

*We **will discuss** this next week.*	*She **is to receive** a medal.*
*I **am going to sell** my boat.*	*The shop **is about to** close.*
*They **are moving** house in October.*	*The train **may be** late.*
*He **leaves** on Friday.*	*It **might** rain.*

The future with *will* or *shall*

You can use the auxiliary verbs *will* and *shall* with the base form of the main verb to express future time:

*I **will send** you a postcard.*   *I **shall send** you a postcard.*

In informal English, especially spoken English, both forms are usually shortened to -'ll: ***I'll send** you a postcard.*

You can also use *will* and *shall* to show determination, insistence, etc.:

*I **will** not give up.*   *She **shall** apologize.*

In formal English, some people express future time with *shall* in the first person (singular and plural) and *will* in the second and third persons:

*I **shall** return*	*we **shall** return*
*you **will** return*	*you **will** return*
*he/she **will** return*	*they **will** return*

and they show determination, insistence, etc., by reversing *will* and *shall*:

*I **will** return*	*we **will** return*
*you **shall** return*	*you **shall** return*
*he/she **shall** return*	*they **shall** return*

This distinction is now considered rather old-fashioned. As early as 1940, Winston Churchill used *shall* in the first person to show determination: 'We shall never surrender.' In modern English both *will* and *shall* are used in all persons, though *will* is the more common of the two.

Sequence of tenses

When you change a verb from the present tense to the past tense, other verbs in the sentence may change too, according to a fixed pattern. This is known as the **sequence of tenses**.

*I **know** it **is** too late.* → *I **knew** it **was** too late.*
*I **think** it **will** rain.* → *I **thought** it **would** rain.*
*I **am** glad I **sold** my house.* → *I **was** glad I **had sold** my house.*

Here is a set of examples involving an *if*-clause:

*If I **want** a car, I **will buy** one.*
*If I **wanted** a car, I **would buy** one.*
*If I **had wanted** a car, I **would have bought** one.*

Aspect

The **aspect** of a verb tells you whether the action or state it refers to is complete or still in progress. There are two aspects, the perfect aspect and the progressive aspect.

The perfect aspect

The **perfect** (or **perfective**) **aspect** consists of the verb *have* followed by a past participle:

*I **have worked** here since 1984.*   *He **had** never **seen** her before.*

In the **present perfect**, the verb *have* is in the present tense (i.e. *has* or *have*). The present perfect expresses an action or state that began in the past and continues up to the present:

*She **has lost** her car keys, so she can't drive home.*

Compare this with the simple past tense, which expresses an action or state that began and ended in the past:

*She **lost** her car keys, so she couldn't drive home.*

(Note that American English often makes use of the simple past where British English has the present perfect. An American may say 'I already ate' or 'Did you read my essay yet?' instead of 'I've already eaten' or 'Have you read my essay yet?')

In the **past perfect**, the verb *have* is in the past tense (i.e. *had*):

*It **had rained** all day.*   *The stains **had disappeared**.*

Some grammars call the present perfect aspect the **perfect tense**, and the past perfect aspect the **pluperfect tense**.

Uses of the perfect aspect

Like the present and past tenses, the perfect aspect may refer to

- a state:

  *She **has been** afraid of spiders since her early childhood.*
  *The book **had been** in the shop window for several months.*

- a habitual action or event:

  *He **has** often **mentioned** your*   *I **had commuted** to London for*
  name.   *many years.*

- a single specific action or event:

    *I **have opened** the door.*   *The firm **had gone** bankrupt.*

The progressive aspect

The **progressive** (or **continuous**) aspect consists of the verb *be* followed by a present participle:

    *I **am watching** television.*   *I **was watching** television.*

In the **present progressive**, the verb *be* is in the present tense (i.e. *am, is,* or *are*). The present progressive expresses an action or state that is continuing or incomplete:

    *He **is living** with his parents.*   *She **is writing** a novel.*

While the simple present often refers to a habitual action, the present progressive may refer to a single event:

    *He usually **wears** a grey jacket for*   *I **play** badminton on Tuesdays.*
    work.   *I **am playing** badminton on*
    *He **is wearing** a brown jacket today.*   *Thursday this week.*

Note also the following oddity, in which the meaning of the verb changes:

    *She **has** a baby.* (i.e. the baby has already been born)
    *She **is having** a baby.* (i.e. the baby has not yet been born)

In the **past progressive**, the verb *be* is in the past tense (i.e. *was* or *were*). The past progressive expresses an action or state that lasted for a period, or that was in progress when something else happened:

    *It **was raining**.*   *We **were sailing** down the river*
                               when the boat capsized.

The perfect and progressive aspects combined

The perfect and progressive aspects are often used together:

    *I **have been working** for this company since 1975.*
    *She **had been listening** to our conversation.*

You can also use them with *will, shall,* or *-'ll* to produce verb phrases expressing future time:

    *By next week he **will have forgotten** all about it.*
    *This time tomorrow I **shall be lying** on the beach.*
    *At the end of September **she'll have been working** for this company*
    for exactly fifteen years.

Negation

Negation is the grammatical process of contradicting or denying the truth of a statement.

The use of *not*

To make a clause or sentence negative you add *not* after the main verb or the (first) auxiliary verb:

*I **am** a psychiatrist.* → *I **am not** a psychiatrist.*
*She **was carrying** a briefcase.* → *She **was not carrying** a briefcase.*
*We **were being** watched.* → *We **were not being** watched.*

Note that if the main verb is anything but *be*, you usually add the auxiliary verb *do* before making the statement negative:

*They **know** your parents.* → *They **do not know** your parents.*
*He **came** home that evening.* → *He **did not come** home that evening.*

In old-fashioned or literary texts, however, you may find *not* after a main verb other than *be*:

... *to die, and go we **know not** where.* (William Shakespeare, *Measure for Measure*, Act III Scene 1)
***Taste not** when the wine-cup glistens.* (Sir Walter Scott, *The Bride of Lammermoor*)

The use of *-n't*

The word *not* is often shortened to *-n't*, especially in informal English:

*You **should accept** their offer.* → *You **shouldn't accept** their offer.*
*They **could have been** delayed.* → *They **couldn't have been** delayed.*

You can add *-n't* to most auxiliary verbs:

are/aren't, is/isn't, was/wasn't, were/weren't, have/haven't, has/hasn't, had/hadn't, does/doesn't, would/wouldn't, should/shouldn't, could/couldn't, might/mightn't, must/mustn't

Sometimes the form or pronunciation of the auxiliary verb changes when you add *-n't*:

do/don't, will/won't, shall/shan't, can/can't

usedn't to or *didn't use to?*

The phrase *used to*, referring to a former state or habitual action, can cause problems when you try to make it negative. Some people treat *used* as a main verb, and make it negative with *didn't*:

> I **used to** walk to work. → I **didn't use to** walk to work.
> He **used to** like whisky. → He **didn't use to** like whisky.

Others treat *used* as an auxiliary verb, and make it negative with *not* or *-n't*:

> I **usedn't to** walk to work.   He **used not to** like whisky.

You may also see or hear:

> I **usen't to** walk to work.   He **didn't used to** like whisky.

Other negative words

A number of other words can be used to make a statement negative.

- the pronouns *nobody, no one, nothing*: He told **nobody** about it.

- the adverbs *nowhere, never*: There is **nowhere** to sit.

- the determiner *no*: There were **no** witnesses.

- the word *neither*: She kept **neither** of her promises.

Most of these words can be replaced with *not* (or *-n't*) + *any, anybody*, etc.:

> He did **not** tell **anybody** about it.   There is**n't anywhere** to sit.
> There were**n't any** witnesses.   She did **not** keep **either** of her
>   promises.

I DIDN'T SAY NOTHING!

This sentence contains a **double negative**, i.e. two negative elements (*-n't* and *nothing*). In theory these cancel each other out, so the sentence actually means 'I said something.' In practice, however, such a sentence is usually intended to mean 'I didn't say anything.' The use of a double negative in this way is unacceptable in standard English.

Sometimes a double negative can be downright confusing. Does the statement *I wouldn't be surprised if it didn't rain* mean that I expect it to rain, or that I expect it not to rain?

There are occasions, however, when it is quite legitimate to use two negative elements in the same sentence:

*We did**n't** tell her **not** to come.*   *We could**n't not** feel sorry for them.*

Formation of verbs

New verbs may be formed in a number of ways. The four most common ways are:

- by adding a fixed ending, called a suffix, to another word:

  soft + -en = soften   *fossil + -ize = fossilize*

- by adding a prefix at the beginning of another verb:

  de- + contaminate = decontaminate   *un- + tie = untie*

(Note that the prefix *de-* can also be added to nouns: *decamp, defrost, debug, detrain,* etc.)

- by joining two or more words together:

  over + estimate = overestimate   *down + grade = downgrade*

- by using a noun as a verb:

  to butter, to captain, to fax, to host, to keyboard, to machine-gun, to microwave, to rubbish, to sandbag, to sandwich, to source, to word

- by using an adverb as a verb:

  *We **downed** tools.*   *Murder will **out**.*
  *They have **upped** their prices.*   *Please **forward** this letter.*

Suffixes forming verbs

The suffixes *-ate, -en, -ify,* and *-ize* may be added to adjectives:

  *domestic**ate**, valid**ate**; deaf**en**, rough**en**; solid**ify**, just**ify**; legal**ize**, standard**ize***

or to nouns:

  *hyphen**ate**, origin**ate**; threat**en**, height**en**; person**ify**, gas**ify**; caramel**ize**, idol**ize***

The suffix *-ize* (sometimes spelt *-ise*) is particularly productive, creating new words that some people love to hate, such as *computerize, containerize, hospitalize, prioritize,* etc.

Note that words ending in *-e* or *-y* drop this letter before the suffix is added:

necessity → necessitate
wide → widen
haste → hasten

pure → purify
beauty → beautify
subsidy → subsidize

Sometimes other letters are dropped, added, or changed:

pollen → pollinate
automatic → automate

identity → identify
stable → stabilize

Complex irregular verbs

Many verbs are formed by adding a prefix or other word in front of an existing verb. If the original verb is irregular, the new verb will have the same irregular endings:

to take, I took, I have taken
to mistake, I mistook, I have mistaken
to overtake, I overtook, I have overtaken
to partake, I partook, I have partaken
to undertake, I undertook, I have undertaken

Here are some more examples:

become, became, become
inlay, inlaid, inlaid
mislead, misled, misled
outshine, outshone, outshone

rewind, rewound, rewound
undo, undid, undone
undergo, underwent, undergone
withstand, withstood, withstood

THIS MESSAGE WILL SELF-DESTRUCT IN FIFTEEN SECONDS

New verbs are sometimes formed by removing the ending from a noun. The verb *self-destruct* comes from the noun *self-destruction*, and the verb *edit* from the noun *editor*. This process is called **back-formation**.

Here are some more examples:

burglar → burgle
sculptor → sculpt
emotion → emote
oration → orate

liaison → liaise
diagnosis → diagnose
enthusiasm → enthuse
television → televise

Compound nouns can also produce new verbs by back-formation:

babysitting → babysit
dry-cleaning → dry-clean

house-hunting → house-hunt
sightseeing → sightsee

Adverbs

What is an adverb?

An **adverb** is a word that tells you when, where, how, why, etc.:

tomorrow, often, here, away, in, out, over, under, slowly, generously

Adverbs may tell you more about:

- a verb: *it was raining **heavily**; they left **yesterday**; we went **in***
- an adjective: ***extremely** cold; **theoretically** impossible; small **enough***
- another adverb: ***quite** well; **very** often*
- a whole clause or sentence: ***Fortunately**, the door was not locked.*
- a noun phrase: *the sky **above**; **rather** a mess*
- a preposition: *just **below** the signature; I haven't seen her **since** then.*

Simple adverbs and compound adverbs

A **simple adverb** consists of a single word: *up, here, sadly, very, often.*

A **compound adverb** consists of two words joined together: *everywhere, somehow, thereupon, hereby.*

Adverbs ending in *-ly*

You can often form an adverb by adding *-ly* to the end of an adjective:

*absolute**ly**, bad**ly**, doubtful**ly**, excited**ly**, free**ly**, great**ly**, surprising**ly***

For most adjectives ending in *-ic* you must add the longer ending *-ally* to form the adverb:

automatic → *automatic**ally***	*energetic* → *energetic**ally***
basic → *basic**ally***	*frantic* → *frantic**ally***

(An exception is *public*, which becomes publicly, not **publically*.)

Sometimes a spelling change is required before you add *-ly*:

easy → *easily*	*comfortable* → *comfortably*
full → *fully*	*true* → *truly*

Adverbs with other endings

Other ways of forming adverbs include:

- adding *-ward* or *wards* to other adverbs: *downward, northwards*
- adding *-ways* to nouns: *sideways, edgeways*
- adding *-wise* to nouns: *clockwise, lengthwise*

Comparative and superlative

Like adjectives (see page 100), many adverbs have comparative and superlative forms with *-er/-est* or *more/most*:

Sam worked **hard**.　　　　　　The branch broke **easily**.
Sue worked **harder**.　　　　　The stick broke **more easily**.
Steve worked **hardest**.　　　　The twig broke the **most easily**.

The **comparative** form (with *-er* or *more*) is used to compare two things: *The stick broke **more** easily than the branch.* The **superlative** form (with *-est* or *most*) is used to compare three or more things: *Steve worked the **hardest** of the three.*

Note that the adverbs *well* and *badly* have the same irregular comparative and superlative forms as the adjectives *good* and *bad*: *well/better/best*; *badly/worse/worst*.

The adverb phrase and the adverb clause

There are three types of phrase or clause that may be used in the same way as an adverb:

- an **adverb phrase**, which consists of a head adverb with other words before and/or after it. In the following examples the head adverb is in bold type:

rather **badly**　　　　　　　　as **often** as possible
strangely enough　　　　　　very **fast** indeed

- an **adverb clause**, which may or may not contain a verb:

He laughed **when he found out**.　We left **because we were bored**.
While washing the car, I noticed　Please come by public transport, **if**
　a dent in the wing.　　　　　　　**possible**.

- a phrase beginning with a preposition:

They live **in London**.　　　　　The helicopter landed **on the roof**.
She waited **for three hours**.　　I cut it **with my knife**.

The term **adverbial** covers all these items – adverbs, adverb phrases, adverb clauses, and prepositional phrases – when they are used as one of the parts of a clause or sentence. You will find more information about the adverbial on page 34.

The position of the adverb

An adverb can sometimes be moved to a different position within a clause or sentence without changing the meaning:

> *Originally* this room may have been used as the kitchen.
> This room *originally* may have been used as the kitchen.
> This room may *originally* have been used as the kitchen.
> This room may have *originally* been used as the kitchen.
> This room may have been *originally* used as the kitchen.
> This room may have been used *originally* as the kitchen.
> This room may have been used as the kitchen *originally*.

> *Slowly* I opened the box.
> I *slowly* opened the box.
> I opened the box *slowly*.

> I closed the door *with a sigh of relief*.
> *With a sigh of relief* I closed the door.

There are, however, some restrictions. You cannot normally put an adverb between a verb and its direct object when the latter is a simple noun phrase: **I opened slowly the box*. And you cannot normally put a phrase or clause used as an adverb between the subject and the verb: **I with a sigh of relief closed the door*.

Changing the position of an adverb may change the meaning of the sentence:

> *Only* Jack washed the car. (i.e. nobody else washed the car)
> Jack *only* washed the car. (i.e. he didn't do anything else)
> Jack washed the car *only*. (i.e. he didn't wash anything else)

> She rejected our offer *sadly*. (= . . . in a sad manner or with feelings of sadness)
> *Sadly*, she rejected our offer. (= it is sad or unfortunate that . . .)

> The children have *naturally* blond hair. (i.e. their hair is not dyed or bleached)
> *Naturally*, the children have blond hair. (= of course, the children have blond hair)

Splitting the infinitive

A **split infinitive** is an infinitive with an adverb between *to* and the main part of the verb:

> to *frankly* admit
> to *officially* announce

> to *easily* close
> to *loudly* explode

The most famous example of the late twentieth century is '... to boldly go where no man has gone before', from the introduction to the television series *Star Trek*.

Some people say that you should never split an infinitive in this way. Most guides to usage, however, advise a common-sense approach. If you can put the adverb before *to* or after the main part of the verb without making the sentence sound awkward or ambiguous, then do so:

> ... **boldly** to go where no man has gone before
> ... to go **boldly** where no man has gone before

However, moving the adverb sometimes makes the meaning unclear:

> They planned to **secretly** exchange the prisoners.
> They planned **secretly** to exchange the prisoners.

The first sentence contains a split infinitive, *to secretly exchange*. But if you move *secretly* before *to exchange*, as in the second sentence, it is not clear whether the adverb relates to the verb *planned* or *exchange*.

Here is another pair of examples:

> They failed to **sufficiently** motivate gifted children.
> They failed to motivate **sufficiently** gifted children.

In the second sentence, does *sufficiently* relate to *motivate* or *gifted*?

Sometimes a split infinitive simply sounds more natural, especially in informal spoken English:

> You're supposed **to partly cook** the vegetables first.

> You need **to really thump** the keys.

SOME OTHER VIEWS ON SPLIT INFINITIVES

The English-speaking world may be divided into (1) those who neither know nor care what a split infinitive is; (2) those who do not know, but care very much; (3) those who know and condemn; (4) those who know and approve; and (5) those who know and distinguish. (H. W. Fowler, *A Dictionary of Modern English Usage*, revised by Sir Ernest Gowers)

... when I split an infinitive, God damn it, I split it so it will stay split. (Raymond Chandler)

I don't split 'em. When I go to work on an infinitive, I break it up in little pieces. (attributed to Jimmy Durante)

Meanings of adverbs

Adverbs and adverbials provide a wide range of information: time, place, manner, reason, degree, etc.

Adverbs of time

Adverbs and adverbials of time, duration, or frequency tell you when, for how long, how often, etc.:

now, then, yesterday, today, tomorrow, this morning, this evening, last week, next year, on Monday, in May, at six o'clock, recently, immediately, soon, later, permanently, temporarily, for three days, during the night, throughout the winter, often, frequently, usually, daily, once a month, always, never

Here are some examples of their use:

*Dinner will be ready **soon**.*
*I'll phone you **this evening**.*
*The film starts **at nine o'clock**.*
*She left **on Sunday**.*
*He died **six months ago**.*

*I haven't seen her **since** 1985.*
*They stayed **for five hours**.*
*It rained **all day**.*
*He **often** misses the bus.*
*She visits her father **every week**.*

Adverbs of place

Adverbs and adverbials of place, position, direction, or distance tell you where, in what direction, how far, etc.:

here, there, somewhere, anywhere, everywhere, nowhere, up, down, in, out, above, below, away, back, at the airport, in Africa, backwards, forwards, north, south, east, west, home, abroad, far, for three miles, ten metres apart

Here are some examples of their use:

*Meet me **at the station**.*
*Bring it **here**.*
*She cycled **across Australia**.*
*He ran **downstairs**.*

*We drove **to the bank**.*
*I sailed **north**.*
*They live **fifty miles away**.*

Adverbs of manner

Adverbs and adverbials of manner, instrument, or agent tell you how, with what, by whom, etc.:

slowly, quickly, happily, sadly, loosely, tightly, loudly, quietly, carefully, casually, subjectively, enthusiastically

Here are some examples of their use:

*She **slowly** opened the door.*   *The children played **happily**.*
*He **reluctantly** agreed to help.*   *Tie the knot **tightly**.*

They also include phrases beginning with *with* or *by*:

*'Good morning,' she said **with a smile**.*
*I killed the wasp **with a rolled-up newspaper**.*
*The process is controlled **by computer**.*
*He was taught music **by his mother**.*

Adverbs of reason

Adverbs and adverbials of reason, result, condition, or concession tell you why, with what result, on what condition, etc.

They include phrases beginning with *of, from, for*, etc., and clauses beginning with *because, (in order) to, so, if, although*, etc.:

*The plants died **from neglect**.*   *I've sprained my ankle, **so I can't***
*I went to the bar **for a drink**.*   **go on the sponsored walk**.*
*We stopped **because we were tired**.* *If it rains*, you'll get wet.*
*They dismantled the engine **to find*** ***Although she was annoyed**, she*
   ***out what was wrong**.*   *told him it didn't matter.*

Adverbs of degree

Adverbs and adverbials of degree or emphasis tell you how much, how little, etc.:

greatly, highly, considerably, deeply, immensely, badly, strongly, completely, utterly, almost, nearly, rather, somewhat, slightly, a little, a bit, hardly, barely

Here are some examples of their use:

*The company has **greatly** increased* *They **badly** need your help.*
  its output.   *The stain has **completely** vanished.*
*I **strongly** object to the proposed* *We **almost** forgot to thank him.*
  bypass.   *My leg hurts **a little**.*
*He **positively** refuses to sell the* *I **hardly** know her.*
  house.

{CONTD}

Other types of adverb

Other adverbs and adverbials include:

- those that express probability, such as *possibly, probably, certainly*:

  *I will **possibly** be late.*
  *He has **probably** forgotten.*

  *This will **definitely** be my last attempt.*

- those that focus or restrict, such as *chiefly, mainly, largely, mostly, especially, particularly, exactly, precisely, just, only, simply, merely*:

  *We **mostly** travel by car.*
  *This is a **particularly** dangerous part of the operation.*

  *That is **exactly** what I want.*
  *I was **only** trying to help.*

- those that tell you what something is concerned with. These are usually phrases beginning with *about, on, over*, etc.:

  *You must be more careful **about** what you spend*.

  *There is a problem **over the will***.

The *wh*-adverbs

The **wh-adverbs** are words like *how, when, where, why, whenever, wherever*, etc., used to ask questions, to introduce relative clauses, to link clauses within a sentence, etc.

***How** did you find out?*
***When** does the concert start?*
*a time **when** fresh vegetables were in short supply*
***Where** should I put this box?*
*the hospital **where** I was born*

***Why** are you wearing gloves?*
*I don't know **why** she left.*
*The dog barks **whenever** a car goes past.*
*He followed her **wherever** she went.*

Intensifiers

An **intensifier** tells you that something is more or less intense, great, strong, etc. Many adverbs can be used to intensify adjectives or other adverbs. Some of the most common ones include:

very, extremely, terribly, desperately, remarkably, thoroughly, completely, absolutely, altogether, too, enough, quite, rather, somewhat, fairly, slightly, a bit, a little, hardly, barely, scarcely

Here are some examples of their use:

very worrying news

I was *extremely* relieved.

He is *desperately* ill.

She played *remarkably* well.

a *thoroughly* unpleasant experience

It was not *altogether* unexpected.

I was driving *too* fast.

Are you *quite* sure?

a *rather* dirty handkerchief

This one tastes *slightly* better.

The words were *barely* legible.

A number of other intensifying adverbs come up time and again with the same adjectives or adverbs:

It is *patently obvious* that she is lying.

The safety precautions were *woefully inadequate*.

I was *bitterly disappointed*.

We are *painfully aware* of our shortcomings.

They were *madly in love*.

WHO EVER TOLD YOU THAT?

The adverb *ever* is sometimes used – especially in informal spoken English – to add emphasis to the *wh*-words *how, when, where, why, what,* and *who*:

How ever did she manage it?

When ever do they have time to do the housework?

Where ever have you been?

Why ever does he need so much money?

What ever is making that noise?

Who ever told you that?

This usage should not be confused with the adverbs *however, whenever,* and *wherever,* and the pronouns *whatever* and *whoever,* which are written as one word:

However hard she tried, she couldn't open the door.

Whenever I hear this song, I think of Simon.

Wherever I hide the presents, the children always find them.

Whatever is making that noise must be outside.

Whoever told you that was pulling your leg.

Adjuncts, subjuncts, disjuncts, and conjuncts

Adverbials can be divided into four categories, according to their use within the sentence. These four categories are:

- adjuncts, the largest group, which relate to the verb or to the whole sentence:

  *Put the clock **on the mantelpiece**.* *He was made redundant **last week**.*
  *She smiled **knowingly**.* *It rained **on Wednesday**.*

- subjuncts, which have a subordinate role:

  ***Politically**, this was not a very wise move.* ***Even** I know how to mend a puncture.*

  *Could you close the door, **please**?*

- disjuncts, which comment on the style or content of the sentence:

  ***Personally**, I don't believe a word of it.* *We are **obviously** wasting our time.*

- conjuncts, which provide a link between clauses, sentences, or paragraphs:

  ***In other words**, she failed.* ***Meanwhile**, he had left the country.*

You may find that other grammar books classify adverbials in different ways, or with different names.

Adjuncts

An **adjunct** relates to the verb or to the whole sentence. The adjuncts form the largest of the four categories of adverbials. They are one of the main elements of a clause or sentence.

Unlike subjuncts, disjuncts, and conjuncts, adjuncts can be used alone in answer to a question:

*She smiled **knowingly**.* *How did she smile? – **Knowingly**.*
*He lives **in a caravan**.* *Where does he live? – **In a caravan**.*
*They are leaving the country **tomorrow**.* *When are they leaving the country? – **Tomorrow**.*

There are two types of adjunct: predication adjuncts and sentence adjuncts.

Predication adjuncts

A **predication adjunct** relates to the verb. It comes at the end of the clause or sentence, which may not be complete without it.

*Put the clock **on the mantelpiece**.   She left the station **in a taxi**.*

You cannot move a predication adjunct to the beginning of the sentence:

*****On the mantelpiece** put the clock.   ***In a taxi** she left the station.*

Sometimes a predication adjunct can be removed altogether:

*She left the station **in a taxi**. → She left the station.*

but sometimes it cannot:

*Put the clock **on the mantelpiece**. (not *Put the clock.)*

Sentence adjuncts

A **sentence adjunct** relates to the whole sentence. It may come at the beginning or end of the sentence, and it can be removed.

*He was made redundant **last week**.   It rained **on Wednesday**.*
***Last week** he was made redundant.   **On Wednesday** it rained.*
He was made redundant.   It rained.

Subjuncts

A **subjunct** has a subordinate role in the sentence. It may

- express a point of view:

  ***Politically**, this was not a very wise move.*
  ***Legally**, she has the same rights as any other employee.*

- express courtesy:

  *Could you close the door, **please**?   **Kindly** refrain from smoking.*

- focus attention on a single word or phrase:

  ***Even** I know how to mend a   They **absolutely** refuse to let us
  puncture.   go.*
  *He sounded **really** unhappy.   She **nearly** lost her job.*

Unlike adjuncts, subjuncts cannot be used alone in answer to a question:

*****Even** they are leaving the country.*
*How are they leaving the country? – *****Even**.*

{CONTD}

Disjuncts

A **disjunct** comments on the style or content of a sentence:

> **Strictly speaking**, you need a licence to operate the radio.
> They were **naturally** eager to hear the results.

Disjuncts usually express a personal opinion of the speaker or writer, and they can be removed:

> You need a licence to operate the radio.
> They were eager to hear the results.

Unlike adjuncts, disjuncts cannot be used alone in answer to a question:

> **Understandably**, they left the country.
> Why did they leave the country? – ***Understandably**.

There are two types of disjunct: style disjuncts and content disjuncts.

Style disjuncts

A **style disjunct** shows how the sentence should be interpreted:

> frankly, to put it bluntly, candidly, in all honesty, to be honest, truthfully, confidentially, privately, between you and me, roughly speaking, broadly, in general, in short, in a nutshell, literally, metaphorically, strictly speaking, personally

Here are some examples of style disjuncts in use:

> **Personally**, I don't believe a word of it.
>
> **To put it bluntly**, the coins are worthless.

Content disjuncts

A **content disjunct** comments on the truth of the sentence, or makes a value judgement about it:

> perhaps, maybe, possibly, probably, most likely, certainly, undoubtedly
> clearly, plainly, obviously, evidently, of course
> basically, essentially, really, actually
> fortunately, luckily, happily, unfortunately, sadly, regrettably
> surprisingly, to our surprise, amazingly, remarkably, curiously, oddly
> naturally, inevitably, understandably, predictably
> thankfully, hopefully
> rightly, wrongly, justly, unjustly, wisely, unwisely, sensibly, foolishly

Here are some examples of content disjuncts in use:

> **Perhaps** she made a mistake.
> They were **naturally** eager to hear the results.

> We are **obviously** wasting our time.
> **Luckily**, the door was not locked.

Conjuncts

A **conjunct** provides a link between clauses, sentences, or paragraphs:

> however, nevertheless, yet, besides, furthermore, moreover, in addition
> therefore, so, consequently, as a result
> namely, for instance, for example, that is
> firstly, secondly, next, finally, last of all
> in conclusion, to summarize, all in all, overall
> alternatively, instead, rather, in other words, on the other hand
> likewise, similarly
> incidentally, by the way, meanwhile

Here are some examples of conjuncts in use:

> There are three things to remember when cooking pancakes. **Firstly**, the pan must be very hot. **Secondly**, . . .
> You can pay by cheque or **alternatively** you can use a credit card.
> She did not reach the required standard; **in other words**, she failed.

Unlike adjuncts, conjuncts cannot be used alone in answer to a question:

> **Meanwhile**, they had left the country.
> When had they left the country? – ***Meanwhile**.

TO TRAVEL HOPEFULLY IS A BETTER THING THAN TO ARRIVE

This famous line from Robert Louis Stevenson's *Virginibus Puerisque* contains the adverb *hopefully* in the sense of 'full of hope'. There are still some people who think that this is the only way in which *hopefully* should be used. In other words, they object to sentences like

> **Hopefully** the rain will stop soon.　　**Hopefully** this is the right key.

in which *hopefully* means 'it is to be hoped that'. There is no common-sense reason why you should not use *hopefully* in this sense, as long as you take care to avoid ambiguity.

Prepositions

What is a preposition?

A **preposition** is a word or phrase that links two parts of a sentence:

over, under, into, out of, before, after, during, in spite of

A preposition often comes after a verb and before a noun phrase:

*She climbed **over** the fence.*   *The bird flew **out of** its cage.*
*He continued **in spite of** our*   *They lived there **before** the war.*
warnings.

The prepositional complement and the prepositional phrase

The words that follow the preposition are called the **prepositional complement**. The preposition and its prepositional complement are together called a **prepositional phrase**.

The prepositional complement may be:

- a noun phrase:

*She climbed over **the fence**.*   *The bird flew out of **its cage**.*
*He continued in spite of **our***   *They lived there before **the war**.*
***warnings**.*

- a pronoun:

*Give it to **me**.*   *This letter is for **you**.*
*I know nothing about **this**.*   *What are you going to do with*
   ***that**?*

- an adverb:

*Is it warm in **there**?*   *I haven't seen him since **then**.*

- a clause beginning with a *wh*-word:

*The house is ten miles from **where***   *Listen to **what he is saying**.*
***she works**.*

The prepositional complement may be another prepositional phrase:

*The dog appeared from **behind the sofa**.*
*He didn't tell her until **after the wedding**.*

If the same preposition has two complements, it is usually not necessary to repeat the preposition:

*I know very little **about** economics or [about] politics.*
*Pay attention **to** what he does and [to] how he does it.*

Preposition or conjunction?

Some words can be prepositions or conjunctions:

*He left **before** midnight.* (preposition)
*He left **before** she arrived.* (conjunction)

*They stayed indoors **until** lunchtime.* (preposition)
*They stayed indoors **until** the rain stopped.* (conjunction)

As a general rule: if the word is followed by a clause that can stand alone as a sentence, then it is a conjunction, not a preposition.

You will find more information about conjunctions in the section beginning on page 196.

Preposition or adverb?

Many words can be prepositions or adverbs:

*I stood **behind** the tree.* (preposition)
*I waited **behind** after the end of the lesson.* (adverb)

*She stepped **off** the pavement.* (preposition)
*She walked **off** without saying goodbye.* (adverb)

The structure of a sentence containing a preposition may be very like that of a sentence where the same word is used as an adverb:

*He sat **on** the chair.* (subject + verb + preposition + noun phrase)
*He switched **on** the radio.* (subject + verb + adverb + noun phrase)

You can sometimes find out whether the word is a preposition or an adverb by trying to move it elsewhere:

He sat the chair **on.* (the preposition cannot be moved)
*He switched the radio **on**.* (the adverb can be moved)

Alternatively, you can try replacing the noun phrase with a pronoun such as *it*. The pronoun comes after the preposition but before the adverb:

*He sat **on it**.*   *He switched **it on**.*

You will find more information about adverbs on in the section beginning on page 172.

{CONTD}

Simple prepositions and complex prepositions

There are two types of preposition: simple prepositions and complex prepositions.

- **simple prepositions** consist of a single word:

  on, off, up, down, in, out, above, below, over, under, to, from, with, without, before, after, at, during, etc.

- **complex prepositions** consist of two or more words:

  according to, ahead of, apart from, as far as, as for, as to, away from, because of, but for, close to, due to, except for, further to, instead of, near to, next to, out of, owing to, regardless of, up to, as well as, by means of, in accordance with, in addition to, in case of, in face of, in favour of, in front of, in spite of, in terms of, in view of, on account of, on behalf of, on top of, with reference to, with regard to, etc.

Do not confuse a complex preposition with two simple prepositions used side by side:

*Wait **until after** Christmas.* (preposition *until* + preposition *after*)

or with an adverb followed by a preposition:

*We went **out for** a walk.* (adverb *out* + preposition *for*)

Note that the phrase *on to* may consist of the adverb *on* + the preposition *to*:

*They drove **on to** the end of the road.*

or just a preposition, now often written as one word:

*They drove **onto** the pavement.*

Ending a sentence with a preposition

You may have heard the 'rule' that a sentence should never end with a preposition. Supporters of this rule insist that a *pre*position should always *pre*cede its complement. But this is sometimes undesirable or impossible:

*He gave me some photographs to look **at**.*

*This seat is not very comfortable to sit **in**.*

*She had forgotten which page she was **up to**.*

*This pen is not easy to write **with**.*

*Was it worth waiting **for**?*

You would not say:

> *He gave me some photographs at *She had forgotten up to which
>   which to look.   page she was.

and the question *Was it worth waiting for?* cannot be expressed in any other way.

However, in formal written English, you can often keep the preposition before its complement without sounding stilted. You could write *one of the women with whom I work* in a formal letter, for example, though you would say *one of the women I work with* when talking to a friend.

You can also sometimes rephrase a sentence to move the preposition from the end:

> *This pen is easy to write **with**.* → *It is easy to write **with** this pen.*
> *This seat is not very comfortable to sit **in**.* → *Sitting **in** this seat is not
>   very comfortable.*

Remember that it is perfectly acceptable to end a sentence with *off, on, in, up,* etc., when these words are functioning as adverbs:

> *I've left the lights on – don't   *When questioned about the story,
>   forget to switch them **off**.*   she confessed that she had
>   made it **up**.*

THIS IS THE SORT OF ENGLISH UP WITH WHICH I WILL NOT PUT

This was Winston Churchill's alleged response to the clumsy English produced by those who go out of their way to avoid ending a sentence with a preposition. Many great writers of the past have broken this 'rule':

And do such bitter business as the day / Would quake to look **on**. (William Shakespeare)

What a fine conformity would it starch us all **into**. (John Milton)

The present argument is the most abstracted that ever I engaged **in**. (Jonathan Swift)

. . . the less convincing on account of the party it came **from**. (Edmund Burke)

. . . too horrible to be trifled **with**. (Rudyard Kipling)

Meanings of prepositions

Prepositions have a wide range of meanings. These include:

- space: *at, to, off, down, from*
- time: *by, until, during before, after*
- cause: *for, because of, on account of*
- manner or means: *without, like*

- accompaniment: *with, without*
- support or opposition: *for, against*
- possession: *of, with, without*
- concession: *despite, in spite of*
- addition or exception: *except, besides, apart from*

Prepositions of space

Prepositions of space form one of the largest groups. They may refer to:

- a position:

  *He works **at** the bank.*
  *Milan is **in** northern Italy.*

  *Her office is **on** the fifth floor.*
  *the bridge **across** the canal*

- one point or position relative to another:

  *She lived **away from** her family for several years.*
  *while the wheel is **off** the car*
  *the car **in front of** the house*
  *Fish cannot survive **out of** water.*
  *the picture **above** the fireplace*
  *the caption **below** the picture*
  *Your slippers are **under** the bed.*

  *the tree **behind** the house*
  *the shop **next to** the bank*
  *the pub **opposite** the church*
  *Tom stood **between** Dick and Harry.*
  *A wild orchid was growing **among** the ferns.*

- movement:

  *She ran **down** the stairs.*
  *He walked **up** the hill.*
  *We drove **across** the bridge.*
  *I cycled **along** the road.*
  *They marched **past** the town hall.*

  *Have you been **through** the Channel tunnel yet?*
  *The plane flew **over** the trees.*
  *The dog crawled **under** the fence.*

- movement towards a point:

  *We drove **to** the station.*
  *Put it **on** the table.*
  *The cat climbed **onto** the roof.*

  *Put it **in** the drawer.*
  *The cat climbed **into** the box.*

- movement away from a point:

*They escaped **from** prison.*　　　*The cat jumped **off** the roof.*
*We drove **away from** the station.*　*Take it **out of** the drawer.*

Prepositions of time

Prepositions of time also have a range of meanings. They may refer to:

- a period of time:

*The strike lasted **for** three months.*　*She introduced many changes*
*You can stay **until** Friday.*　　　　　　**during** *her term of office.*
*He has been here **since** eight o'clock*　*It rained **throughout** the night.*
　this morning.

- a point in time:

*He arrived **at** six o'clock.*　　　*We should be home **by** midnight.*
*She left **on** Thursday.*　　　　　*They are getting married **in** June.*

- one point in time relative to another:

*Elizabeth arrived **before** William.*　　*three days **after** Christmas*

DIFFERENCES OF OPINION

Which is the 'correct' preposition to use after *different*? Should you say
different from, different to, or *different than*? This has long been a contro-
versial issue, and there are still many people whose teeth are set on edge
by *different to* or *different than*. The short answer is that none of the
three is 'incorrect', but *different from* is the least likely to cause offence.

Those who favour *different from* and condemn *different to* often do
so on the grounds that the verb *differ* takes the preposition *from* – you
say *this one differs from that one*, not **this one differs to that one*. But
adjectives do not always follow the same pattern as the verbs from which
they are derived.

The phrase *different than* is more frequent in American English, and
some British people dislike it for this reason alone. However, it is sometimes preferable to *different from* when followed by a clause:

*My taste in music is different **from** yours.* but *My taste in music now is different*
　than *it was twenty years ago.*

{CONTD}

Other prepositions

Other prepositions include:

- prepositions of cause:

  *He retired early **because of** ill health.*
  *She is angry on **account of** what you said.*
  *I went back to work **out of** necessity.*
  *They have been punished **for** their crimes.*
  *This offer is targeted **at** the unemployed.*

- prepositions of manner or means:

  *We've been working **like** slaves all day.*
  *He was disguised **as** a woman.*
  *I prefer to travel **by** train.*

  *She nudged him **with** her elbow.*
  *We found our way **without** any difficulty.*

- prepositions of accompaniment:

  *Lindsay arrived **with** her brother.*

  *Don't go **without** me!*

- prepositions of support or opposition:

  *How many people voted **for** him?*
  *She always sides **with** the underdog.*

  *I'm **against** the proposal.*

- prepositions of possession:

  *the roof **of** the house*
  *a chair **with** a broken leg*

  *a drug **without** any side-effects*

- prepositions of concession:

  *They continued **despite** my warning.*
  *She had a good time, **in spite of** the weather.*

  ***Notwithstanding** our objections, the council demolished the building.*

- prepositions of addition or exception:

  *We have two other cars **besides** this one.*
  *You don't need to wear a jacket **as well as** a jumper.*
  *Nobody **but** Steven was late.*

  *Everything **except** the television belongs to my flatmate.*
  *All these towns, **apart from** Cherbourg, are in Germany.*

Prepositions with more than one meaning

Many prepositions have more than one meaning:

The helicopter landed **on** the roof.
They arrived **on** Wednesday.
a book **on** photography
Would you spend fifty pounds **on** a bottle of wine?

It depends **on** the weather.
She was acting **on** my instructions.
He lived **on** bread and water for several weeks.
Play the tune **on** the piano.

I'll meet you **at** the station.
They laughed **at** us.
It is cooked **at** a high temperature.

The doctor left **at** four o'clock.
He was disappointed **at** the result.
She's good **at** maths.

He lives **with** his parents.
She is not popular **with** her employees.

I hit it **with** a hammer.
The children screamed **with** delight.
a room **with** a view

They left **for** the airport.
How much did you pay **for** this computer?

We waited **for** two hours.
She gave me a car **for** my birthday.
a cure **for** cancer

Prepositions in phrases and idioms

Prepositions are used in a wide range of figurative phrases and idioms:

across the board
against the grain
at arm's length
below the belt
beyond the pale
by fair means or foul
from bad to worse

in a spot
near the knuckle
off the hook
out of one's depth
over my dead body
under the counter
with open arms

a shot **in** the arm
a chip **off** the old block

a pat **on** the back
a millstone **round** someone's neck

to hope **against** hope
to breathe **down** someone's neck
to be par **for** the course
to start **from** scratch
to cut **off** one's nose to spite one's face

to jump **on** the bandwagon
to throw someone **off** the scent
to let the cat **out of** the bag
to paper **over** the cracks
to pay **through** the nose
to bark **up** the wrong tree

Conjunctions

What is a conjunction?

A conjunction is a word or phrase that links two clauses or other parts of a sentence:

and, or, but, when, while, if, unless, although, because, so

There are two types of conjunction: coordinating conjunctions and subordinating conjunctions.

Coordinating conjunctions

A **coordinating conjunction** (or **coordinator**) links parts of a sentence that have the same status, such as two main clauses, two noun phrases, two adjectives, two adverbials, etc. The three 'central' coordinating conjunctions are *and, or,* and *but.* (There are also a number of 'marginal' coordinating conjunctions, including *then* and *yet.*)

Here are some examples of the use of *and, or,* and *but*

- between main clauses:

  *Peter has a cat **and** Anne has a dog.*   *I speak French **but** I don't speak*
  *You can walk **or** you can go by bus.*   *German.*

- between noun phrases:

  *She bought a packet of crisps **and***   *Would you like tea **or** coffee?*
  a can of lemonade.   *I have two brothers **but** no sisters.*

- between adjectives:

  *The weather was cold **and** damp.*   *We were tired **but** happy.*
  *The plant has pink **or** white flowers.*

- between adverbials:

  *He ran out of the garden **and** across*   *'No thank you,' she replied politely*
  the road.   **but** *firmly.*
  *Did you pay in cash **or** by cheque?*

Linking more than two items

The conjunctions *and* and *or* may link more than two items:

*I've invited Mike **and** Sue **and** Paul **and** Chris.*
*You can have tea **or** coffee **or** wine **or** beer.*

In such cases, you usually replace all but the last conjunction with commas:

I've invited Mike, Sue, Paul, and Chris.
You can have tea, coffee, wine, or beer.

(The comma after *Paul* and *wine* is optional.)

Sometimes, however, you may wish to keep all the conjunctions for effect:

*I've made the beds **and** done the ironing **and** cleaned the windows **and** mown the lawn – can I have a rest now?*
*You can watch television **or** play in the garden **or** do some painting **or** play a game **or** read a book – just don't tell me you're bored!*

Subordinating conjunctions

A **subordinating conjunction** (or **subordinator**) links parts of a sentence that do not have the same status. The subordinating conjunction usually comes at the beginning of a subordinate clause used as an adverbial. (You will find more information about subordinate clauses in the section 'Subordination' on page 206.)

There are many subordinating conjunctions, with a wide range of meanings: *when, before, after, while, since, until, where, if, in case, although, whereas, except, because, for, in order that,* etc. Here are some examples of their use at the beginning of a subordinate clause:

*We left **when** it began to rain.*
***Before** you joined the company, I was the only graduate on the staff.*
*She called **while** we were out.*

***If** I post it today, you should get it tomorrow.*
*Bring your cheque book **in case** they don't take credit cards.*

Note that the subordinate clause sometimes comes at the beginning of the sentence.

Correlatives

Some conjunctions are used in pairs. These are called **correlatives**. The following pairs are **coordinating correlatives**: *both ... and; either ... or; neither ... nor; not only ... but also*

***Both** Mike **and** Pete have relatives in Australia.*
*You can **either** withdraw the money after five years **or** reinvest it.*

The following pairs are **subordinating correlatives**: *if ... then; scarcely/hardly ... when; more/less ... than; so/such ... that*

***If** x is 4, **then** 5x must be 20.*
***Scarcely** had I sat down **when** the phone rang.*

Meanings of conjunctions

Coordinating conjunctions

The coordinating conjunction *and* usually expresses addition or combination:

*I've invited Mike **and** Sue.*
*She bought a red **and** black dress.*

*His father is a teacher **and** his mother is a doctor.*

In such cases, you can usually change the order of the parts linked by *and*:

*I've invited Sue **and** Mike.*
*She bought a black **and** red dress.*

*His mother is a doctor **and** his father is a teacher.*

However, *and* may also link two things that happen one after the other:

*He ran out of the garden **and** across the road.*
*She fell down the stairs **and** broke her leg.*

In such cases, the order of the parts cannot be changed:

He ran across the road **and out of the garden.*
She broke her leg **and fell down the stairs.*

The coordinating conjunction *or* expresses a choice or alternative:

*Would you like tea **or** coffee?*
*Is the car new **or** second-hand?*

*We usually watch television **or** listen to music in the evenings.*

The coordinating conjunction *but* expresses a contrast:

*We were tired **but** happy.*
*He has many acquaintances **but** few friends.*

*She recharged the battery **but** the car still wouldn't start.*

Subordinating conjunctions

The subordinating conjunctions have a wide range of meanings.

- *when, before, after, as, while, since, till, until,* etc., express time:

*We left **when** it began to rain.*
***As** I opened the door, I heard a strange noise.*

*He has lived alone **since** his wife died.*
*Wait **till** the boss finds out!*

- *where, wherever,* etc., express place:

*We must go **where** the jobs are.*

*You can sit **wherever** you like.*

- *because, as, since, for*, etc., express a reason:

  We sold the car **because** it cost too much to run.
  As she has no children, the money will go to her nieces and nephews.
  He turned away, **for** he was embarrassed.

(Note that *for* is rather formal or old-fashioned, and you are most likely to come across it in literature.)

- *so that, in order that, to, in order to*, etc., express a purpose:

  He stood up **so that** she could sit down.
  In order to renew your passport, you must fill in this form.

- *so* expresses a result:

  I felt cold, **so** I closed the window.

- *if, as long as, providing, unless, in case*, etc., express a condition:

  If we run, we may catch the early train.
  Bring your cheque book **in case** they don't take credit cards.

- *although, though, if, even if*, etc., express concession:

  Although she lives in the same road, we rarely see each other.
  I'm determined to finish this, **if** it takes me all week.

- *whereas, while, whilst*, etc., express contrast:

  Janice is good at maths, **while** her brother has a flair for languages.

- *except (that)* expresses exception:

  I'd love to come, **except (that)** I've promised to babysit for Lisa.

- *as, as if, as though, like*, etc., express similarity or comparison:

  Are you taking more exercise, **as** the doctor advised?
  It sounds **as though** he's not happy in his new job.

Note that some subordinating conjunctions have more than one meaning:

  The door creaked **as** I opened it.   He never does **as** he is told.
  She left early, **as** she was tired.

You will find more information about conjunctions in the section 'Coordination and subordination' on page 204.

Sentence structure

Simple sentences and multiple sentences

A **simple sentence** consists of a single clause:

It snowed all day.   *I borrowed my brother's car.*
She ran across the road.   *We have a problem.*

You will find more information about the structure of simple sentences in the section 'Sentences – the basics' beginning on page 28.

A **multiple sentence** contains more than one clause:

Alan works in insurance and Jane is a college lecturer.
They speak French but they don't speak German.
Mike cooked the dinner while Sally had a bath.
If it rains we can go to the cinema.

Main clauses and subordinate clauses

There are two types of clause used in multiple sentences: main clauses and subordinate clauses. A **main clause** (or **independent clause**) is like a simple sentence – it sounds complete:

Alan works in insurance   *I speak French*
Jane is a college lecturer   *I don't speak German*
Mike cooked the dinner   *we can go to the cinema*

A **subordinate clause** (or **dependent clause**) cannot stand alone as a sentence – it sounds incomplete:

while Sally had a bath   *if it rains*

You will find more information about subordinate clauses in the section 'Subordination' on page 206.

Compound sentences and complex sentences

Multiple sentences come in two varieties: complex sentences and compound sentences. A compound sentence contains two or more main clauses. A complex sentence contains a main clause and a subordinate clause.

Compound sentences

A **compound sentence** contains two or more main clauses linked by *and, or, but,* etc.:

Alan works in insurance | *and* | *Jane is a college lecturer.*
You can go by car | *or* | *you can take the train.*

*They speak French | **but** | they don't speak German.*

If both main clauses have the same subject, the subject may be left out of the second main clause:

*She closed the window | **and** | [she] drew the curtains.*
*He read the article | **but** | [he] didn't understand it.*
*You can go by car | **or** | [you can] take the train.*

(Note that in the last example the auxiliary verb *can* is also left out of the second clause.)

You can usually change the order of the main clauses, but the coordinating conjunction must remain in the middle:

*Alan works in insurance | **and** | Jane is a college lecturer.*
*Jane is a college lecturer | **and** | Alan works in insurance.*

*You can go by car | **or** | you can take the train.*
*You can take the train | **or** | you can go by car.*

When a compound sentence contains more than two main clauses, this is called **multiple coordination**:

Alan works in insurance | and | Jane is a college lecturer | and | I am a nurse.

Complex sentences

A **complex sentence** contains a main clause and a subordinate clause beginning with a word like *when, while, before, after, if, although,* etc.:

*Mike cooked the dinner | **while** Sally had a bath.*
*They arrived at the station | **after** the train had gone.*

The subordinate clause sometimes comes first:

***Before** you joined the company | he was the only graduate on the staff.*
***As** she opened the door | she heard a strange noise.*

Compound-complex sentences

A **compound-complex sentence** contains at least two clauses linked by *and, or, but,* etc., and at least one subordinate clause.

Mike cooked the dinner | and | Kate laid the table | while Sally had a bath.
My grandfather died | after my parents got married | but | before I was born.

In the first example the word *and* links two main clauses. In the second example the word *but* links two subordinate clauses.

Coordination and subordination

The parts of a sentence may be joined together in two ways, by coordination or subordination.

Coordination

Coordination occurs between parts of a sentence that have the same status, such as two main clauses, two noun phrases, two adjectives, two adverbials, etc. These parts are linked by a coordinating conjunction or coordinator (i.e. *and, or, but*).

- coordination between main clauses:

  Peter works in insurance and Anne is a college lecturer.
  I speak French but I don't speak German.

(Clauses linked in this way are called **coordinate clauses**.)

- coordination between noun phrases:

  *Would you like **tea or coffee**?*   *I have **two brothers but no sisters**.*

- coordination between adjectives:

  *The weather was **cold and damp***   *We were **tired but happy**.*

- coordination between adverbials:

  *He ran **out of the garden and across the road**.*
  *'No thank you,' she replied **politely but firmly**.*

You can often change the order of the parts linked by a coordinating conjunction:

  Peter works in insurance and Anne is a college lecturer. or *Anne is a college lecturer and Peter works in insurance.*
  *Would you like **tea or coffee**?* or *Would you like **coffee or tea**?*
  *'No thank you,' she replied **politely but firmly**.* or *'No thank you,' she replied **firmly but politely**.*

You will find more information about coordinating conjunctions in the section 'Conjunctions' beginning on page 196.

Linked coordination and unlinked coordination

When two or more parts of a sentence are linked by coordinating conjunctions, this is called **linked coordination** (or **syndetic coordination**):

*The children were **cold and tired and hungry**.*

If commas or other punctuation are used in place of coordinating conjunctions, this is called **unlinked coordination** (or **asyndetic coordination**):

*The children were **cold, tired, hungry**.*

Segregatory coordination and combinatory coordination

There are two types of coordination in which noun phrases are linked by *and*: segregatory coordination and combinatory coordination.

In **segregatory coordination**, the noun phrases can be separated to form two clauses:

***Mark and Ruth** live in Scotland. → Mark lives in Scotland and Ruth lives in Scotland.*

In **combinatory coordination**, the noun phrases form a single unit and cannot be separated:

***The president and the prime minister** met to discuss the crisis. (not *The president met to discuss the crisis and the prime minister met to discuss the crisis.)*

AND SO TO BED

There is nothing ungrammatical about using the conjunctions *and* and *but* to link two sentences, especially for dramatic effect or emphasis. Many great writers of the past have done so:

The curate faced the laurels – hesitatingly. **But** Aunt Maria flung herself on him. (Kenneth Grahame, *The Golden Age*)

True and False are attributes of speech, not of things. **And** where speech is not, there is neither Truth nor Falsehood. (Thomas Hobbes, *Leviathan*)

Sentimentally I am disposed to harmony. **But** organically I am incapable of a tune. (Charles Lamb, *Essays of Elia*)

News is what a chap who doesn't care much about anything wants to read. **And** it's only news until he's read it. (Evelyn Waugh, *Scoop*)

{CONTD}

Subordination

Subordination occurs between parts of a sentence that do not have the same status. In the following examples, the subordinate parts are in bold type:

> We left **when the show was over**. Tell me **what you think**.
> I broke my tooth **while eating an apple**.
> The book **that I bought yesterday** is on the shelf.

Subordinate clauses

There are several types of **subordinate clause**, with a variety of uses. You can use a subordinate clause in place of any of the main elements of a sentence (apart from the verb):

- as the subject

  What you need is a more powerful computer.
  That her father is a lawyer is of no relevance.

- as the direct object

  I don't know **where she lives**.   He asked me **why I was leaving**.

- as the indirect object

  Please tell **whoever is making that noise** to stop it at once!

- as the complement

  Her theory was **that he would try to leave the country**.
  This is **what I am looking for**.

- as subject *and* complement

  What you see is **what you get**.
  What I meant was **that I don't mind**.

- as the adverbial

  I broke my ankle **when I fell down the stairs**.

(When a subordinate clause is used as an adverbial it begins with a subordinating conjunction or subordinator. You will find more information about these in the section 'Conjunctions' beginning on page 197.)

You can also use a subordinate clause as *part of* one of the main elements of a sentence:

- after a noun, as part of the subject or object

*The dog **that bit me** belongs to my neighbour.*
*She is suing the man **who sold her the car**.*

(You will find more information about this type of clause in the section 'Relative clauses' on page 88.)

- after a preposition

  *He gave us some advice on **what we should do next**.*

- after an adjective

  *She was reluctant **to tell us her name**.*

In most of the above examples, the subordinate clause is a finite clause. In other words, it contains a verb in the present or past tense:

*what you **need***	*when I **fell** down the stairs*
*that her father **is** a lawyer*	*that **bit** me*

A subordinate clause may also be a non-finite clause. In other words, it may contain the infinitive or one of the participles (the *-ing* form or *-ed* form) of a verb:

*She was reluctant **to help**.*
*They had an accident **while driving home**.*
***Evicted from his flat**, he lived on the streets.*

You will find more information about finite clauses and non-finite clauses on page 143.

Multiple subordination

Multiple subordination occurs when one subordinate clause contains another subordinate clause.

*She knows || **that she will fail her exams** | **if she doesn't work harder**.*

In this example, the subordinate clause *that she will fail her exams if she doesn't work harder* is the object of the verb *knows*. This clause contains a subordinate clause of its own, *if she doesn't work harder*.

Here are some more examples:

*He showed us || **what he was doing** | **when the accident happened**.*
***If you lose your passport** | **while you are abroad** || you should contact the police.*

Comparative clauses

You use a **comparative clause** when you are comparing people or things:

> Jack is **older than I am**.
> She makes **more phone calls than you do**.
> Computers are **less expensive than they used to be**.
> This car uses **less petrol than that one does**.

The comparative clause has two parts, a comparative element (e.g. *older, less expensive*) and a subordinate clause beginning with *than* (e.g. *than I am, than they used to be*).

The comparative element

The **comparative element** usually contains an adjective ending in *-er* or a phrase beginning with *more* or *less*.

For comparison to a higher degree you use *-er* or *more*:

> This book is **cheaper** than the one you bought.
> The north has a **colder** climate than the south has.
> She is **more talented** than her father was.
> The school has **more pupils** now than it had fifty years ago.
> He drives **more carefully** than his sister does.
> You have **more** than I have.

For comparison to a lower degree you use *less* (or *fewer* for plural nouns):

> This book is **less expensive** than the one you bought.
> I had **less time** than I thought I had.
> Our parents had **fewer opportunities** than we have.
> He responded **less enthusiastically** than she did.
> A mouse eats **less** than a cat does.
> Both of them made mistakes, but Jack made **fewer** than Sarah.

The comparative element may be

- an adjective or adjective phrase: *cheaper, more talented, less expensive*
- a noun phrase: *a colder climate, more pupils, less time, fewer opportunities*
- an adverb or adverb phrase: *more carefully, less enthusiastically*
- a pronoun: *more, less, fewer*

You will find more information about comparison on page 100.

Equivalence and non-equivalence

Comparisons to a higher or lower degree are comparisons of **non-equivalence**. In other words, the things you are comparing are not the same. Comparisons to the same degree – when the things you are comparing are the same – are comparisons of **equivalence**. They use the structure *as . . . as . . .*:

> She is **as talented as her father was**.
> I have **as much money as I need**.
> Hold your breath for **as long as you can**.

Similes and some other idiomatic phrases are comparisons of equivalence:

> The water was **as clear as crystal**.
> This bag is **as light as a feather**.
> Her two sons are **as different as chalk from cheese**.
> I'm up by seven o'clock **as often as not**.

> The outlook is **not as black as it is painted**.
> The questions were **as easy as they come**.
> It's **as true as I'm sitting on this camel**.

Ellipsis in comparative clauses

You can often drop part of a comparative clause if it repeats something you have already said:

> It was easier than we expected [it to be].
> I have more friends now than [I had] five years ago.
> This pan holds less than that one [holds].
> The pain is as bad as [it has] ever [been].

Dropping or leaving out part of a clause is called ellipsis. You will find more information about ellipsis on page 213.

MORE BY GOOD LUCK THAN GOOD JUDGEMENT

When we say that something happened *more by good luck than good judgement*, we usually mean that a lot of luck and little or no judgement was involved.

Similarly, we sometimes use *more than* to mean 'very' or *less than* to mean 'not at all':

> You are **more than** welcome to stay.
> We were **more than** surprised to hear that she was getting married.

> He was **less than** pleased to see us.
> They were **less than** willing to help.

Comment clauses

A **comment clause** is a short clause that you add to show your attitude to what you are saying:

> *you see; I think; mind you; what's more; to be honest*

Comment clauses are mainly used in speech, rather than in writing. They may come at the beginning, middle, or end of the sentence:

> ***What's more**, they didn't even apologize.*
> *It's too wide, **you see**, so it won't fit in the gap.*
> *We don't really need a second car, **to be honest**.*

Comment clauses are parenthetical. In other words, you can remove them from the sentence without affecting the structure:

> *They didn't even apologize.*   *It's too wide, so it won't fit in the*
> *We don't really need a second car.*   *gap.*

Types of comment clause

A comment clause usually contains a verb. Here are some of the most common patterns:

- subject + verb: *I know; I think; I suppose; I must say; you know; you see; they say; it seems; it's said; God knows*

- subject + verb + complement: *I'm afraid; I'm sorry to say; you'll be glad to hear*

- *as* + subject + verb: *as I said; as I've explained; as you know; as you may remember; as it happens*

- clauses beginning with *what*: *what's more; what is strange; what is hard to understand*

- clauses containing a present participle (i.e. the *-ing* form of a verb): *putting it bluntly; generally speaking; strictly speaking*

- clauses containing a past participle (i.e. an *-ed* form or irregular equivalent): *put bluntly; put simply; roughly translated*

- clauses beginning with an infinitive (with *to*): *to put it bluntly; to be frank; to be fair; to coin a phrase; not to put too fine a point on it*

Uses of comment clauses

You can use comment clauses for a variety of purposes:

- to express certainty

  *It won't be easy, **I know**.*   ***I must say**, he's a good cook.*
  She has the right qualifications,   *You are well aware, **I'm sure**, that*
      ***it's true**.*   *this is illegal.*

- to express a tentative opinion, report a rumour, etc.

  *We could try writing to his old address, **I suppose**.*
  *The price includes VAT, **I think**, but not delivery.*
  *Henry VIII slept here, **I'm told**.*

- to express a frank opinion

  ***Putting it bluntly**, your services are no longer needed.*
  *I don't care, **to be honest**.*

- to express hope, regret, relief, annoyance, etc.

  *She hasn't changed her mind, **I hope**.* *He didn't miss the train, **I'm glad***
  *You're too late, **I'm afraid**.*   ***to say**, but it was a close thing.*

- to explain or make something clearer

  *We couldn't find the key, **you see**,* ***To put it simply**, the battery is*
    so we tried to pick the lock.   *flat.*

- to draw the attention of the listener

  As you know**, his wife is a lawyer.* *It sounds tempting, **you must
                                  ***admit**.*

FILLING A GAP

What a queer thing Life is! So unlike anything else, don't you know, if you see
   what I mean. (P. G. Wodehouse, *My Man Jeeves*)

We often use comment clauses like *you know, you see, I mean*, etc., in
a fairly meaningless way – to fill a gap, to give ourselves time to think,
or simply out of habit:

*It has a sort of flat bit at the back, **you know**, that you can put your feet on.*
*I only asked for ten pounds – **I mean** they're not exactly short of money, are they?*

Shortening the sentence

There are two ways in which you can shorten a sentence to avoid repeating a word or phrase:

> *I peeled the apple and ate it.* (= I peeled the apple and ate the apple.)
> *She asked him to close the door but he didn't.* (= She asked him to close the door but he didn't close the door.)

The first example avoids repeating *the apple* by using *it* in place of the phrase. The word *it* is called a pro-form. The second example avoids repeating *close the door* by leaving out the phrase. This is called ellipsis.

Pro-forms

A **pro-form** is a word that you use in place of a longer word or phrase. The most common type of pro-form is the pronoun, used in place of a noun or noun phrase:

> *The caretaker closed the door and locked **it*** [= the door].
> *This ring was the most expensive **one*** [= ring] *in the shop.*

Pro-forms may also be adverbs, or words like *do*, *so*, etc. These may be used in place of adverbials, verbs, or clauses:

> *I drove to the station and left my car **there*** [= at the station].
> *Ben worked harder than Sue **did*** [= worked].
> *Is it still raining? – I think **so*** [= that it is still raining].

Co-reference and substitution

Pro-forms have two different uses: co-reference and substitution. In **co-reference**, the pro-form refers to exactly the same thing: *I looked for **my pen**, but I couldn't find **it***. In **substitution**, the pro-form simply replaces another word or phrase: *I looked for **a pen**, but I couldn't find **one***.

Pro-forms used in co-reference include:

- pronouns such as *he, her, myself, themselves,* etc.

  > ***Caroline** said **she** would be late.*   ***The bear** scratched **itself**.*

- adverbs such as *here, there, then*

  > *I stopped off **at the newsagent's** and bought a paper **there**.*
  > *You'll see him **on Saturday** and you can tell him **then**.*

Pro-forms used in substitution include:

- pronouns such as *one, some, several, another,* etc.

    *She had a photo of Alan and Kate, and **several** of the new baby.*
    *He arrived in one car and left in **another**.*

- the verb *do*

    *They are playing better than they have ever **done**.*
    *Emma sometimes walks to work, but Jack never **does**.*

- adverbs such as *so, the same, similarly, likewise,* etc. (often with *do*)

    *Is it still raining? – I think **so**.*   *He sat on the floor and the children*
    *She likes opera and **so do** I.*   **did the same**.
    *If I offer to pay half, will you **do***
    ***likewise**?*

Ellipsis

When you leave out part of a sentence, this is called **ellipsis**: *We thought we'd solved the problem but we hadn't* [solved the problem].

Ellipsis is often used in everyday speech:

    Glad you like it. (= *I'm glad you like it.*)
    Serves him right. (= *It serves him right.*)
    Pleased to meet you. (= *I'm pleased to meet you.*)
    Anyone want another cake? (= *Does anyone want another cake?*)

It is also used in dialogue:

    What are you doing? – [I'm] *Washing my hair.*
    Where are my car keys? – [They are] *On the table.*
    When will you be back? – *I don't know* [when I will be back].
    Who broke this glass? – *Lisa* [broke it].

Cataphoric ellipsis and anaphoric ellipsis

Ellipsis usually refers backwards to something that has already been mentioned. This is called **anaphoric ellipsis**: *We thought we'd solved the problem but we hadn't* [solved the problem].

However, it sometimes refers forwards to a later part of the sentence. This is called **cataphoric ellipsis**: *Unless you need to* [open the windows], *it's advisable not to open the windows in an air-conditioned room.*

{CONTD}

Ellipsis in multiple sentences

If a sentence contains two main clauses with the same subject, you can usually leave out the subject of the second clause:

He closed the window and [he] *drew the curtains.*
She read the magazine and [she] *threw it away.*

But if a sentence contains a main clause and a subordinate clause with the same subject, you cannot leave out the subject of the second clause:

He closed the window because he was cold. (not **He closed the window because was cold.*)
She read the magazine while she waited for the bus. (not **She read the paper while waited for the bus.*)

Recoverability

When you shorten a sentence using ellipsis or a pro-form, it should be obvious what has been left out or what the pro-form refers to. In other words, the missing text should be **recoverable**.

In **textual recoverability** you can find the missing word or words elsewhere in the text:

I went to the post office and then [I went] *to the library.*
*The caretaker closed the door and locked **it*** [= the door].

In **situational recoverability** you can work out what is missing from the situation – who is speaking, what they are pointing at, etc.:

[I'm] *Glad you could come.*
*Does **this*** [= this scarf, bag, etc.] *belong to you?*

In **structural recoverability** you can use your knowledge of grammatical structure to work out what is missing:

Jenny was going to come but [she] *changed her mind.*
[The] *Vicar who left* [his] *wife for* [his] *curate* [is] *still in* [his] *job*[.]
    (newspaper headline)

Contraction

Contraction occurs when you shorten a word like *not, is, are, have,* etc., and attach it to the word before. This is another way of shortening a sentence in informal speech or writing. The short form, also called a contraction, has an apostrophe in place of the missing letters. Here are some of the most common contractions:

- *am* → *'m*: *I'm not coming with you.*
- *is* → *'s*: *She's going to America.*; *What's the matter?*
- *are* → *'re*: *You're my best friend.*; *We don't know where we're going.*
- *has* → *'s*: *He's never been there before.*; *It's got no wheels!*
- *have* → *'ve*: *I've no idea.*; *He should've told her.*
- *had* → *'d*: *I'd no idea.*; *We thought it'd stopped raining.*
- *will* → *'ll*: *They'll never find us.*; *That'll be the day.*
- *would* → *'d*: *I thought he'd fail.*; *Who'd have thought it?*
- *not* → *n't*: *It isn't easy.*; *You shouldn't have told them.*

(See page 166 for other examples of *n't*.)

Note that *is* and *has* are both shortened to *'s*, and *had* and *would* are both shortened to *'d*. You can usually work out what the full form should be from what follows the contraction.

In speech, you can sometimes combine *'d* and *'ve*, *'ll* and *'ve*, etc.:

> Who**'d've** thought it?
> They**'ll've** forgotten all about it by tomorrow.

A common error in writing is to put *of* in place of *'ve*, because they sound the same:

> You should**'ve** checked the times of the trains. (not *You should **of** checked the times of the trains.)

IF IT AIN'T BROKE, DON'T FIX IT

The contraction *ain't* is chiefly used in informal speech, especially in American English and in some dialects of British English. It is not generally acceptable in standard English. It may be short for *am not*, *is not*, *are not*, *has not*, or *have not*:

I **ain't** crazy.	Things **ain't** what they used to be.
The opera **ain't** over till the fat lady sings.	She **ain't** seen him for days.
	You **ain't** heard nothing yet!

Other contractions used colloquially or in dialects of English include:

dunno (= don't know)	innit (= isn't it)
gonna (= going to)	geddit? (= Do you get it?)
wanna (= want to or want a)	

Emphasis

When you speak, you can often change the meaning of what you say by putting the emphasis on different words. In the following examples, the emphasized words are in bold type:

> *I* *didn't see the police car, but Mike did.*
> *I* ***didn't*** *see the police car, honestly!*
> *I didn't* ***see*** *the police car, but I heard its siren.*
> *I didn't see the* ***police*** *car, but I saw the car it was chasing.*
> *I didn't see the police* ***car***, *but I saw a police van.*

Given information and new information

A sentence often contains two types of information: given information and new information. The **given information** is something you already know (i.e. information that you have already been given). The **new information** is something you do not know (i.e. something new). When you speak a sentence containing both types of information, you usually put the emphasis on the new information.

Here is a question followed by an answer containing given information and new information:

> *Where did you go skiing? – We went skiing* ***in Austria***.

In this answer, *we went skiing* is the given information and *in Austria* is the new information. The person asking the question knows that you went skiing, but doesn't know where.

Here is the same answer with a different question:

> *What did you do in Austria? –* ***We went skiing*** *in Austria.*

This time, *we went skiing* is the new information and *in Austria* is the given information.

In everyday conversation, of course, you would answer the question with just the new information:

> *Where did you go skiing? – In Austria.*
> *What did you do in Austria? – We went skiing.*

Rearranging the sentence for emphasis

In speech or writing, you can also change the emphasis by rearranging the parts of a sentence. There are several ways in which you can do this.

Existential *there*

You can emphasize a whole clause or sentence by putting *there* at the beginning. Such sentences are described as *existential*, because they tell you that something exists:

No carpet was on the floor. → **There** *was no carpet on the floor.*
A number of theories exist. → **There** *exist a number of theories.*

Note that in these sentences the word *there* does not have its usual meaning of 'in, at, or to that place'.

Existential *there* does not always come at the beginning of the sentence, as in the opening line of J. R. R. Tolkien's *The Hobbit*:

In a hole in the ground there lived a hobbit.

In everyday language, existential *there* is most often used with the verb *be*:

There is *too much money at stake.*   **There was** *a horse in the stable.*
There are *a few cakes left.*   **There were** *five names on the list.*

Note that the verb agrees with the subject of the original sentence:

A few cakes are *left.* → *There* **are a few cakes** *left.* (not *There **is** a few cakes left.)
Five names were *on the list.* → *There* **were five names** *on the list.* (not *There **was** five names on the list.)

However, in informal speech you may sometimes hear *there's* used in place of there are:

There's *a few cakes left – does anybody want one?*

Fronting

Fronting is moving something to the front of a sentence to make it stand out. The part you move to the front is a part that doesn't normally go there, such as the adverbial, complement, or object:

She ran down the hill. (subject + verb + adverbial)
Down the hill *she ran.* (adverbial + subject + verb)

It was terrifying. (subject + verb + complement)
Terrifying *it was.* (complement + subject + verb)

They told us a pack of lies. (subject + verb + object)
A pack of lies *they told us.* (object + subject + verb)

You can even move part of a verb phrase to the front:

He won't apologize. → **Apologize** *he won't.*

{CONTD}

Inversion

Inversion is changing the order of subject and verb. This often occurs at the same time as fronting. The subject usually moves to the end of the sentence:

> *The sun came out.* (subject + verb + adverbial)
> *Out **came the sun**.* (adverbial + verb + subject)
>
> *Mary's exam results were even more disappointing.* (subject + verb + complement)
> *Even more disappointing **were Mary's exam results**.* (complement + verb + subject)

Sometimes the subject moves into the middle of the verb phrase:

> *I have warned him many times.* → *Many times **have I warned** him.*

Cleft sentences

In a **cleft sentence** you change a simple sentence into a multiple sentence by splitting it into two clauses:

> *Jane was playing the piano.* → *It was Jane | who was playing the piano.*
> *The handle is broken.* → *It is the handle | that is broken.*
> *He prefers the blue one.* → *It is the blue one | that he prefers.*
> *We sold the house in June.* → *It was in June | that we sold the house.*

The first clause begins with *it is* or *it was*, followed by the part of the sentence that you want to emphasize. The second clause usually begins with *that*, *who*, or *whom*.

You can change the emphasis by putting different parts of the sentence into the first clause:

> *I left my umbrella on the train.*
> *It was **I** who left my umbrella on the train.*
> *It was **my umbrella** that I left on the train.*
> *It was **on the train** that I left my umbrella.*
>
> *David saw Julie last Sunday.*
> *It was **David** who saw Julie last Sunday.*
> *It was **Julie** whom David saw last Sunday.*
> *It was **last Sunday** that David saw Julie.*

In a **pseudo-cleft sentence**, the emphasized part comes at the end. You draw attention to it with a *what*-clause at the beginning:

You need a holiday. → *What you need is a holiday.*
We would like to know who is responsible for this. → *What we would
    like to know is who is responsible for this.*
I switched the engine off first. → *What I did first was switch the engine
    off.*

Extraposition

Extraposition involves moving a clause to the end of a sentence for
emphasis. The clause is often the subject of the original sentence. In the
new sentence you replace the clause with *it*:

Why she left is a mystery. → *It is a mystery why she left.*
That he has no experience doesn't matter. → *It doesn't matter that he
    has no experience.*
Moving house can be very stressful. → *It can be very stressful, moving
    house.*

The clause is not always the subject of the original sentence:

I didn't say finding a job would be easy. → *I didn't say it would be easy,
    finding a job.*
They warned me that travelling alone could be dangerous. → *They
    warned me that it could be dangerous, travelling alone.*

IT'S THE THOUGHT THAT COUNTS

Proverbs and other fixed phrases often use emphasis for effect. Here are
some examples of cleft sentences:

It's the thought that counts.   *It's an ill wind that blows nobody
It's a long road that has no   any good
    turning.*   *It's dogged as does it.*

And here are some of extraposition:

It's no use crying over spilt milk.   *It's a woman's privilege to change
It's good to talk.   her mind.*

Reporting speech

There are two ways in which you can express what someone has said: direct speech and indirect speech.

In **direct speech** you repeat the actual words used:

> Mandy said, 'I'm not sure.'
> 'It doesn't matter,' replied Pete.
> 'You're too late,' they told us.
>
> She asked, 'Where should I sit?'
> 'I don't need any help,' he said impatiently.

In **indirect speech** (or **reported speech**) you change the words:

> Mandy said that she was not sure.
> Pete replied that it didn't matter.
> They told us that we were too late.
>
> She asked where she should sit.
> He said impatiently that he didn't need any help.

In both types of speech the sentence is made up of two clauses: the reporting clause and the reported clause.

The **reporting clause** contains a subject, a verb of speaking or writing, and any extra information:

> Mandy said
> replied Pete
>
> they told us
> he said impatiently

The **reported clause** contains what was said or written. In direct speech this is usually a sentence in quotation marks (also called inverted commas). In indirect speech it is usually a subordinate clause beginning with *that* or a *wh*-word:

> 'I'm not sure.'
> 'It doesn't matter,'
> 'Where should I sit?'
>
> that she was not sure
> that it didn't matter
> where she should sit

Changing direct speech to indirect speech

You have to make a number of adjustments when you change direct speech to indirect speech.

- the reporting clause remains the same, but you usually move it to the beginning of the sentence:

> 'You're too late,' **they told us**. → **They told us** that we were too late.

Note that when the subject comes after the verb in direct speech, you move it back to its normal place before the verb for indirect speech:

'It doesn't matter,' **replied Pete**. → **Pete replied** *that it didn't matter.*

- in the reported clause, you usually change the verb (from present to past, from past to past perfect, etc.):

She said, 'I **have** *no idea.'* → *She said that she* **had** *no idea.*
I replied, 'I **threw** *it away.'* → *I replied that I* **had thrown** *it away.*
He asked, 'When **will** *it be ready?'* → *He asked when it* **would** *be ready.*

In some special cases, the tense of the verb does not change:

If she says, 'I **want** *to help,' you must let her.* → *If she says that she* **wants** *to help, you must let her.*

- also in the reported clause, you often change personal pronouns (from *I* to *he* or *she*, from *we* to *they*, from *you* to *I* or *we*, etc.):

*Mandy said, '***I***'m not sure.'* → *Mandy said that* **she** *was not sure.*
*'***I*** don't need any help,' he said impatiently.* → *He said impatiently that* **he** *didn't need any help.*
*'***You***'re too late,' they told us.* → *They told us that* **we** *were too late.*

- also in the reported clause, you sometimes have to change references to time or place:

He said, 'I called **yesterday** *but there was no reply.'* → *He said that he had called* **the day before** *but there was no reply.*
She said, 'You can't stay **here***.'* → *She said that I couldn't stay* **there***.*

- if the reported clause is a question, you have to make certain structural changes (e.g. from verb + subject to subject + verb, by adding *if* or *whether*, etc.):

She asked, 'How old **is the car***?'* → *She asked how old* **the car was***.*
He asked, 'Is it possible?' → *He asked* **if** *it was possible.*

The reported clause in indirect speech

In indirect speech the reported clause is a subordinate clause that usually begins with *that* or a *wh*-word:

He said **that he would write to you***.*
I asked **which hotel they were staying in***.*

You can usually drop the word *that* from the beginning of a reported clause, but you cannot drop a *wh*-word:

He said **he would write to you***.* (but not **I asked* **hotel they were staying in***.)*

{CONTD}

222 • Sentence structure

Punctuating direct speech

When you write direct speech, you usually put the reported clause in quotation marks (also called inverted commas). Traditionally, you put a comma after the reporting clause if it comes first:

> Mandy said, 'I'm not sure.'   I asked, 'How much will it cost?'

If the reported clause comes first, you usually put a comma before the closing quotation marks (unless the reported clause is a question or exclamation, in which case it has a question mark or exclamation mark):

> 'It doesn't matter,' replied Pete.   'Where do you live?' she asked.
> 'You're too late,' they told us.   'Go away!' he shouted.

The reporting clause in direct speech

In direct speech the reporting clause may come at the beginning, in the middle, or at the end:

> **I said**, 'If it rains, we can go bowling instead.'
> 'If it rains, we can go bowling instead,' **I said**.
> 'If it rains,' **I said**, 'we can go bowling instead.'

Note that if the reported clause contains two sentences, the punctuation is different:

> 'I don't know what to do,' I said. 'This has never happened before.'

Inversion

When the reporting clause comes in the middle or at the end, the subject sometimes comes after the verb. This is called **inversion**:

> 'If it rains,' **said Pete**, 'we can go bowling instead.'
> 'I'm not sure,' **replied Mandy**.

But if the subject is a personal pronoun, it usually stays before the verb:

> 'If it rains,' **he said**, 'we can go bowling instead.' (not *said he)
> 'I'm not sure,' **she replied**. (not *replied she)

You will sometimes see *said he, said she, said I*, etc., in literature – especially in older texts – but these forms are not in general use.

Dropping the reporting clause

In stories and novels, when the writer is reporting a conversation between two or more characters, the reporting clause is often omitted once the identity of the speakers has been established:

> Simon was still up when Jan got home.
> 'Where have you been?' he asked.
> 'None of your business.'
> 'I was worried – you've never been this late before.'

Free indirect speech and free direct speech

In literature, indirect speech is sometimes presented without a reporting clause. This is called **free indirect speech**:

> Simon was furious with Jan. Where had she been all evening, and what had she been doing?

In ordinary indirect speech, this would be:

> Simon was furious with Jan. He asked her where she had been all evening, and what she had been doing.

Free direct speech, which has no quotation marks or reporting clause, is also used in literature, but less frequently than free indirect speech. It is usually a way of presenting someone's thoughts:

> I walked through the deserted town centre. This must be one of the dullest places on earth. What am I doing here?

In ordinary direct speech, this would be:

> I walked through the deserted town centre. 'This must be one of the dullest places on earth,' I thought. 'What am I doing here?'

IT'S NOT WHAT YOU SAY, IT'S THE WAY THAT YOU SAY IT

In fiction, journalism, and other writing, people often do not simply *say* something. They may utter it in hundreds of different ways. (According to David Crystal, in *The Cambridge Encyclopedia of the English Language*, nearly 600 substitutes for *said* were found in a study of 100 twentieth-century novels.) Here are just a few of the possibilities:

bark, growl, snarl, roar, thunder, gush, coo, sigh, yawn, drawl, murmur, mutter, whisper, laugh, chuckle, sneer, sob, wail, whimper, howl, . . .

Above the sentence

Connecting sentences

Most sentences do not stand alone. When you write or speak English, you usually link your sentences together to form running text in which the meaning of individual sentences often depends on what has gone before.

You can use a variety of words and phrases to connect sentences:

- pronouns

  *My father is coming tomorrow. **He** should be here by lunchtime.*
  *My car wouldn't start. **It** had a flat battery.*

- adverbial words and phrases

  *Mary went home at three o'clock because she didn't feel well. **Two hours later**, she was rushed to hospital with suspected appendicitis.*
  *I set off for the supermarket. **Halfway there**, I realized that I'd left my purse at home.*
  *Your problem may be caused by a dietary deficiency. **In other words**, you are not eating enough of the right food.*

- words like *do, so,* etc.

  *The weather forecast said it might rain this weekend. I hope it **doesn't**.*
  *Paul asked you to phone the plumber. Have you **done so**?*

- a noun phrase beginning with *the, this, that,* etc.

  *A letter and a postcard lay on the mat. **The letter** was addressed to Sue.*
  *You may hear a series of high-pitched bleeps. **This sound** indicates that the machine is malfunctioning.*

- a coordinating conjunction

  *We begged the doorman to let us in. **But** he refused.*
  *Caroline and I had a row at the party. **And** I haven't seen her since.*

- an expression of comparison

  *She has three sons. Michael is the **eldest**.*

- word and phrases like *the former, the latter,* etc.

  *The company is launching two new models this year, the Famiglia and the Veloce. **The former** is an estate car, **the latter** is a coupé.*

Sometimes the linking word refers to the whole of the previous sentence:

*When we finally got to the airport, we found that the flight had been
cancelled. **That** was the last straw!*
*They leave the central heating on all the time, even when they're away.
It's a terrible waste of fuel.*

Paragraphs

In writing, sentences are usually linked together to form paragraphs. A
paragraph is a group of sentences relating to the same topic, event, etc. –
it is not a grammatical unit, and there are no rules as to how long or short
it should be.

Here is what Sir Winston Churchill said about paragraphs in his book
My Early Life:

> Just as the sentence contains one idea in all its fullness, so the paragraph
> should embrace a distinct episode; and as sentences should follow one
> another in harmonious sequence, so paragraphs must fit onto one
> another like the automatic couplings of railway carriages.

In writing, typing, etc., you always start a new paragraph on a new line.
You leave a space at the beginning of the new line (or above it) to show
that this is not just a new sentence.

DO WE SPEAK IN SENTENCES?

In everyday conversation, we often link our thoughts together without
breaking them up into conventional sentences. Here is a transcript of
someone's spoken account of traffic problems on the M6 motorway:

*. . . when we got to the junction with the M6 there was a sign saying the
motorway was closed at Junction 17 but we kept going . . . we thought it might be
clear by the time we got there . . . remember that time we were going to Scotland
and they said there was a hold-up near Carlisle and we just drove straight through
. . . anyway it wasn't . . . the traffic just ground to a halt and everyone switched off
their lights and just sat there . . . it was like a great big car park . . .*

Here is the same account, set out in writing as part of an informal letter.
The words are virtually the same, but punctuation has been added:

*When we got to the junction with the M6 there was a sign saying the motorway
was closed at Junction 17. But we kept going – we thought it might be clear by
the time we got there. (Do you remember that time we were going to Scotland
and they said there was a hold-up near Carlisle but we drove straight through?)
Anyway, it wasn't. The traffic ground to a halt and everyone switched off their
lights and just sat there: it was like a great big car park!*

Intonation and stress

When you speak, you vary the sound of your voice to add meaning to what you say. Such changes include pitch, loudness, speed, or rhythm – or any combination of these. Intonation and stress are important because they give clues about the grammatical structure of what you are saying.

Intonation

Intonation is varying the pitch of your voice to show that you are asking a question, to express emotion, etc. Intonation in speech often serves the same purpose as punctuation in writing.

Asking a question

When you ask a question, the pitch of your voice usually rises towards the end of the sentence: *Is it raining?* This is particularly important when the sentence has the grammatical form of a statement rather than a question:

> *You're leaving tomorrow?*   *She's lost her key?*

(Note that the intonation of a question is represented in writing by a question mark.)

Making a list

When you list things out loud, the pitch of your voice usually falls on the last item. The following list is incomplete, and the pitch remains high: *I've looked in the drawer, on the shelf, under the bed, . . .*

(Note that the intonation of an incomplete list is represented in writing by a set of three dots, also called an ellipsis.)

The following list is complete, and the pitch falls on *go swimming*: *You can play tennis, use the gym, have a round of golf, go swimming.*

Expressing emotion

Varying the pitch of your voice often affects the meaning of what you say, or the way a remark is interpreted. For example, try saying the following sentence in a way that shows genuine appreciation, then change your intonation to suggest sarcasm or anger:

> *That's a great help!*

Stress

Stress is saying a word (or part of word) more loudly to draw attention to it. In all the examples below, the stressed part of the word or sentence is in bold type.

Stress on part of a word

In English words of two or more syllables, the main stress usually falls on the same syllable every time you say the word. In everyday speech you always say *happiness, reversing, confused,* etc. – you never say **happiness, *reversing,* or **confused.*

However, there are a number of words that have different stress or pronunciation when they are used in different word classes. Here are a few examples:

*con**flict*** (verb) / ***con**flict* (noun)   *in**sert*** (verb) / ***in**sert* (noun)
*pre**sent*** (verb) / ***pres**ent* (noun or   *re**cord*** (verb) / ***re**cord* (noun)
   adjective)   *re**fuse*** (verb) / ***ref**use* (noun)

Some words have more than one stress pattern in the same word class:

*dis**pute*** (verb or noun) / ***dis**pute* (noun)
*ex**port*** (verb) / ***ex**port* (verb or noun)

Using stress to make a distinction

You can use stress to distinguish between two things that sound similar:

*I said I saw a **black bird**, not a **black**bird – I think it was a crow.*
*The original expression was 'a **fine**-tooth **comb'**, not 'a fine **tooth**comb'.*

In doing this, you sometimes put the stress on parts of words that are not normally stressed:

*These contributions are paid by the employ**er**, not the employ**ee**.*
*Are the goods to be **im**ported or **ex**ported?*

Stress on part of a sentence

You can change the meaning of a sentence by putting the stress on different words:

Mary *never forgets my birthday.*   *Mary never forgets **my** birthday.*
*Mary **never** forgets my birthday.*   *Mary never forgets my **birthday**.*

You will find more information about this in the section 'Emphasis' on page 216.

Punctuation

Punctuation is the use of commas, semicolons, apostrophes, question marks, etc., for grammatical or other purposes. Without punctuation, most written or printed texts would be difficult or impossible to understand.

she knocked the boy off his bicycle and drove on without stopping the boy who was not hurt reported the incident to the police they are now looking for the car a white estate car which may have been stolen

Punctuation can also change the meaning of the same string of words:

These are my daughters.   *The story he told me is not true.*
These are my daughter's.   *The story, he told me, is not true.*

The comma

The **comma** (,) is probably the most versatile of all the punctuation marks. Here are some of its most important uses.

- after each item in a list:

  They have four cats, two dogs, a rabbit, and a goldfish.
  You can go sailing, swimming, windsurfing, or water-skiing.

(Note that the commas before *and* and *or* can be omitted.)

- before and after a phrase or clause that can be left out without affecting the grammatical structure of the sentence:

  Tom Davis, a former employee of the company, was accused of setting fire to the factory.
  This ring, which belonged to my grandmother, is very valuable.

For the use of commas in clauses beginning with *which, who,* etc., see page 89.

- between clauses:

  If you don't know what the word means, look it up in a dictionary.
  He had eaten four rounds of sandwiches and a packet of biscuits, and he was still hungry.

Note that you only need a comma between clauses when the sentence would be awkward or unclear without one. In the following example the comma is needed to avoid ambiguity:

I didn't want her to go, because I felt unwell.

The use of the comma is often a matter of personal taste or common sense. Some people will write *a dull, cold, rainy afternoon*, while others prefer *a dull cold rainy afternoon*. Neither is incorrect. However, a comma should not be used to separate a subject from its verb:

> *The player with the highest score at the end of the game is the winner.*
> (not **The player with the highest score at the end of the game, is the winner.*)

The semicolon

The **semicolon** (;) is chiefly used between two main clauses:

> *The snow fell steadily throughout the night; in the morning the road was impassable.*

You could split this compound sentence into two simple sentences:

> *The snow fell steadily throughout the night. In the morning the road was impassable.*

Or you could replace the semicolon with the coordinating conjunction *and* – with or without a comma:

> *The snow fell steadily throughout the night, and in the morning the road was impassable.*

Semicolons are also sometimes used in lists, especially when one or more of the items already contains a comma:

> *She is the author of several novels, mostly science fiction; six plays, two of which have been adapted for television; a collection of poems, the most famous being 'Why me?'; and an autobiography.*

The colon

The **colon** (:) is used between two main clauses when the second clause explains or otherwise expands on the first:

> *I have a confession to make: I forgot to post the letter.*
> *He was very worried: she had never been so late before.*

You can also use a colon to introduce a list:

> *You will need the following tools: a hammer, a screwdriver, a spanner, and a drill.*
> *Only five students passed the exam: Michael Green, Kate Brown, Anna White, Jonathan Black, and Peter Grey.*

{CONTD}

The full stop

The **full stop** (.) is used to mark the end of a sentence. It has no other grammatical function.

However, full stops are also used after some abbreviations:

e.g., i.e., a.m., p.m., etc., Co. (= Company), Oct. (= October)

Note that a full stop is not needed if the abbreviation contains the last letter of the word (*Mr, Mrs, St, Dept, Ltd*), and metric units of measurement should never have full stops (*kg, km, cm, ml*).

The apostrophe

The **apostrophe** (') has two main functions in grammar:

- to show possession

  This is my son's car.
  These books are Sarah's.

  One of your duties is to carry the guests' luggage up to their rooms.

- to show that something is missing

  It's still raining.

  She didn't hear him.

The use of an apostrophe in the plural forms of numbers and single letters is optional and increasingly unfashionable:

in the 1990's

to mind your p's and q's

It is also disappearing from the names of commercial institutions:

Lloyds Bank

Pears Cyclopedia

The hyphen

The **hyphen** (-) is used in some compound nouns, adjectives, etc.:

forget-me-not, eye-opener, red-haired, mind-boggling

It is also used to break a word at the end of a line, especially in printed texts:

The castle, built around 1500, was badly damaged by fire in the seventeenth century. It was restored by the great-grandfather of the present owner, . . .

Other punctuation marks

- the **question mark** (?) is used at the end of a question:

  Where do they live?   *You've sold your car?*

- the **exclamation mark** (!) is used at the end of an exclamation or interjection:

  What a shame!   *Ouch!*

- quotation marks (' ' or " "), also called **inverted commas**, are used in pairs around direct speech, quotations, etc.:

  'It has never happened before,' she said.
  The word 'accommodate' is often misspelt.

- **brackets** (), also called **parentheses**, are used in pairs around something that can be left out without affecting the grammatical structure:

  Mr Jones (the girl's father) complained to the council.

- the **dash** (–) is sometimes used instead of a colon:

  I have a confession to make – I forgot to post the letter.

You can also use a pair of dashes in the same way as a pair of brackets:

  Mr Jones – the girl's father – complained to the council.

- a set of three dots (. . .), also called an **ellipsis**, is used to show that something is missing:

  They need food, water, clothing, bedding, . . .
  Jack and Jill went up the hill . . . And Jill came tumbling after.

NEED I SAY MORE?!

The exclamation mark can be used to turn any statement, or even a question, into an exclamation.

There was mud all over the carpet!   *She denied everything!*
The money had disappeared!   *What could I say?!*

Good writers, however, take care not to overuse the exclamation mark:

Cut out all those exclamation marks. An exclamation mark is like laughing at your
  own joke. (F. Scott Fitzgerald)
So far as good writing goes, the use of the exclamation mark is a sign of failure. It
  is the literary equivalent of a man holding up a card reading LAUGHTER to a
  studio audience. (Miles Kington)

Index

A page number in bold type indicates the main reference for items that have more than one reference. Entries in the Quick-reference guide to grammatical terms (pages 1-16) are not referred to in this index.